ON the EDGE of the
ABSURD

ON the EDGE of the ABSURD

LANCE WEBB

↻

ABINGDON PRESS   NEW YORK   NASHVILLE

ON THE EDGE OF THE ABSURD

Copyright © 1965 by Abingdon Press

Library of Congress Catalog Card Number: 65-14721

Scripture quotations unless otherwise noted are from the
Revised Standard Version of the Bible, copyrighted 1946
and 1952 by the Division of Christian Education, National Council of Churches, and are used by permission.

Certain scripture passages, indicated by NEB, are from
The New English Bible, New Testament. © The Delegates
of the Oxford University Press and The Syndics of the
Cambridge University Press 1961. Reprinted by permission.

SET UP, PRINTED, AND BOUND BY THE
PARTHENON PRESS, AT NASHVILLE,
TENNESSEE, UNITED STATES OF AMERICA

TO all sincere unbelievers, as well as believers, who are seeking to make the ultimate test of experience, I dedicate this book;

TO all who from time to time have momentary glimpses of the absurdity of faith and the greater absurdity of unfaith;

TO all honest doubters who by their doubt pay tribute to the deeper possibilities of faith;

TO all who think and must choose between their thoughts which ones to give their ultimate concern—

TO you I address these thoughts and experiences of mine and of the noblest persons I have known

PREFACE

Not so long ago it was easy for man to believe he was master of everything. Now the mood of our times is one of cynicism and doubt—often carefully concealed—that man is really the master of anything! We no longer dream and write of bright utopian futures except in the realms of science and material progress. Here anything is still possible and likely.

The big question is not whether we may develop technically a society of abundance and order where all human needs are met, but whether we are capable of the moral and spiritual character required to create and sustain it.

In the personal realm, the question is not for most of us whether we can make a living even with a reasonable amount of luxury, but whether we can find a meaning that transcends the absurdities of boredom, emptiness, lovelessness, and death.

This is not only an age of anxiety. It is also an age of disillusionment and frustration. We have been subjected to the absurdities of an age of science with all its potential glories that has exploded into an age both of revolution and moral degeneracy. For most of us have knowledge about everything except the things that matter most: the meanings and values, the purposes and resources by which life at its best is possible.

I too am a child of this age. I have faced these absurdities in my own experience. I have shared them with thinking persons in all walks of life. I have met the specters of unbelief on college and university campuses where I have sought to minister over the past twenty-five years. I am qualified, at least, to speak on the edge of the absurd!

Am I also qualified to write about the precious faith that gives the courage to live, the power to care responsibly and to die victoriously? You will be the judge for yourself. But remember, you have no authentic, "scientific" basis for judgment until you have not only sought to understand the witness that is declared here, of those who have lived by such faith in the Reality they call God, but also until you have tested that faith in your own experience.

Do you think this a dogmatic statement? Or do you recognize the narrow way of testing the evidence of any truth as the way of experience, whether in a laboratory with test tubes or in the more complex human laboratory of thinking, desiring, and willing existence?

Most of these considerations were first shared in an attempt to communicate my convictions with the people of my own congregation. They took much of their present shape as the Willson Lectures given at McMurry College in November, 1962, and again as the Religion-in-Life Lectures at Baldwin-Wallace College in January, 1964.

I am grateful to James M. Willson, whose generous gifts

have made the Willson Lectures possible through twenty-three foundations on twenty college and university campuses in this country; to President H. Gordon Bennett of McMurry College; to President A. B. Bonds and Chaplain Edwin Moore of Baldwin-Wallace College for their encouragement in the completion and publishing of this work; and to my daughter Ruth, whose questioning mind has been a stimulus to my own attempt to face the ever present doubts of our age.

I am thankful for the help of my faithful secretary, Doris Cowgill, who has so patiently and efficiently worked with the manuscript and the references.

An old saying sticks in my mind: "Knowledge comes with willingness, power from obedience!"

Yours for the willingness of an open mind and the obedience to the highest that alone produces life.

LANCE WEBB

CONTENTS

the LOSS of MY
AUTHENTIC SELF

We all live and love, suffer, and die on the edge of the absurd. The word "absurd" describes our human dilemma quite well, for it means "contrary to reason," "inconsistent," "foolish," "farcical." Frequently life and its costly sacrifices seem meaningless, irrational, "foolish," even "farcical."

This human absurdity has been often expressed in modern art, drama, poetry, and music. Some schools of existentialism have made a philosophy of life out of it. In the theater of the absurd, everything that takes place on the stage expresses the silly irrationalities and inconsistencies of human life. For instance, two men come out on the stage and play the piano, but end up by tearing it to pieces and throwing the pieces into the audience! Silly? "Yes," they say, "but so is life. Better to be an honest beatnik than a dishonest square!" While most of us do not go to these extremes, in our more thoughtful moments we too are conscious of the ridiculous incongruities of our situation.

How absurd is man's life!

Longing for infinite knowledge, our understanding is still finite. Only barely have we touched even the edges of our universe. Priding ourselves on our intelligence, we are often mocked by the abysmal ignorance of the things that matter most. This is true in medicine or the other sciences and certainly in the field of human relations.

Living in time, we long to be timeless. Demanding life that never ends, we confront the abyss of death which seems to end all.

Therefore the perennial question, "Who am I?" never seems to get an adequate answer. Today this question, though absurd, is necessary if we are to have the courage to live in this wonderful but disturbing time. More progress physically and materially has been made in the last five years than in any other fifty years since the time of Copernicus. Indeed, we have witnessed a breathtaking breakthrough into the vast mysteries of space, electronics, and the atom. We talk of the bigness of the universe. Our imaginations reel and stagger before the impossible picture of billions of galaxies larger than ours in infinite space. And we try to match the bigness of our universe by the bigness of our machines, including some big H-bombs. We brag about the indescribable destruction that could be wrought in a few minutes to any "aggressor," knowing full well the same devastation would rain on us.

The important question is: How big are our spirits? Are we

big enough morally and spiritually to handle the physical power we have in our hands? Many people are afraid we are not. Others try to forget it all and get on with their little game of fun- and money-making. Some hide their heads in the sands and say "after me the deluge," as they do little to prevent it. Others are overwhelmed by the absurdity and rebel in irrational acts or lose hope altogether. Either approach is absurd because it keeps them from living at their best in the world as it is.

The answer to it all, if there is an answer, depends on our faith. And we all have a faith, whether or not we call it that, as every golf player has a stance, his way of approaching the ball. So our faith is really the stance, the way we approach life, or what Paul Tillich calls "our ultimate concern." Of course, the golfer must commit himself to use this stance. He must hit the ball squarely and then follow through. So our faith stance requires commitment and disciplined follow-through.

What is my stance? My ultimate concern in life? My approach to this ultimate question of who I am?

Am I a bit of atomic dust going it blind? Do I belong to an accidental collocation of atoms that strangely, mysteriously produced a Beethoven, a Christ, a Hitler, a Nero, and at last has produced me? Am I nothing more than "a sick fly taking a dizzy ride on the wheel of an impersonal universe"? "A vertical vertebra with a perfect sewage system"?

Or am I a son of God with eternity in my heart so that these values to which I give myself are in the very nature of reality?

All of these answers are symbolic descriptions which are being given to the question of who I am. Which is nearer the truth and how can I know?

15

METHODS OF SELF-KNOWLEDGE

There are several ways of finding out who I am.

First we have *the method of common sense observation.* We begin by realizing that each of us is, at best, a complex bundle of contradictions. A battle is going on within us most of the time. "Man is a Civil War," said Walt Whitman. As one man put our ancient but modern dilemma:

> Within my earthly temple there's a crowd;
> There's one of us that's humble, one that's proud,
> There's one that's broken-hearted for his sins,
> There's one that unrepentant sits and grins;
> There's one that loves his neighbor as himself,
> And one that cares for naught but fame and pelf.
> From much corroding care I should be free
> If I could once determine which is me.[1]

Surely this is our biggest practical problem as well as philosophical: "If I could once discover which is me."

How much indeed everyone of us would give to be his authentic self! But it is not as easy as the little old lady in the Mother Goose rhyme seems to indicate. When she became confused, she said rather comfortingly to herself:

> I've a little dog at home, and he'll know me;
> If it be I, he'll wag his little tail,
> And if it be not I, he'll loudly bark and wail.

It would be a relief indeed if you and I could carry such a little dog in our pockets, so that when we are fulfilling our authentic selves the dog would "wag his tail"; and when we are not, as much of the time we are not, he would bark and he would wail. Unfortunately, life is not quite that simple.

Second there is *the way of philosophy*. The great thinkers and philosophers of all the great religions in all ages have sought an answer. The Greeks have a legend that the ancient oracle at Delphi first spoke the counsel, "Know thyself." Socrates taught that "the proper care of the soul, leading to the good life requires self knowledge," but this knowledge is not primarily general information, however exhaustive, about man's physical, mental and emotional make up; but a true modesty concerning what he knows and does not know, about what he is and is not and that this knowledge can be found by diligent study meditation and prayer.

Gautama, the rich young Indian prince back in 560 B.C., who became the Buddha, was heir to a rajah's throne, but gave it up in order to find out who he was. Like others, for a while he had escaped the questions concerning the meaning of existence by giving over to pleasure and indulgence. One day he gave up these things and for two years sought in solitude and in the teaching of wise men to find the answer. At last as he sat under the Bodhi tree rapt in meditation, he had a series of tremendous spiritual experiences which brought him illumination. He began to teach and practice what he called "The Four Noble Truths" which would help a person understand himself and his sufferings. The essence of his way (which we call Buddhism) is that existence is suffering; suffering is caused by attaching ourselves to the desires of this life; and we overcome this false craving by the noble eightfold path: right belief, right aims, right speech, right actions, right occupation, right endeavor, right thinking, right meditation.

17

Today we have a renaissance of Buddhism all over the world. On many of our American college and university campuses, there are intelligent people dedicated to what they call Zen Buddhism. While there are certainly helpful elements in this approach, to some of us this is not a method of finding the answer but of escaping the problem, as will be indicated later on in this chapter.

A third way very popular in recent years is *the psychological approach*. Modern psychology, beginning with Sigmund Freud, is dedicated to helping us know ourselves. We are in trouble, say the psychologists, because we really don't want to know who we are. We are afraid of what we will find. So we rationalize and justify ourselves in keeping the things we think we desire, while remaining ignorant of the real values, the things we need and really want most. The only way we will ever know who we are is to get rid not just of our ignorance about ourselves, but of our will to ignorance!

A fourth way is *the way of intelligent faith* based on the experience of mankind and our own experience. True, much that is helpful in our quest for self-knowledge is found in all of these other ways; but there is one person who has done more to help us find out who we are than any other: the man Jesus, whom we as Christians call Christ the Lord. Many of us with our Christian heritage have grown up with at least a secondhand belief in Christ, but such belief has never become a living, vital faith, the stance by which we live. As we widen our knowledge of other stances, we find ourselves filled with an honest and necessary doubt. It is very necessary for all of us to ask: What difference does faith in Christ make in discovering this precious knowledge of ourselves?

18

Obviously the first answer is: little or no difference that is valuable. Many who profess this faith are no different from, no better than, those who don't. Indeed, as the old Negro spiritual says of the people of Jesus' time, They crucified him because "they didn't know who he was." No wonder, they did not know who *they* were.

And yet, an objective view of Christian history, in spite of the horrors perpetrated in the name of Christ, will reveal that many of the mountain peak personalities, whose contributions have blessed and enriched human life, lived by their faith in Christ. Certainly the ones I most admire and most desire to be like were among those committed to the Christian faith.

But what do we mean by the stance of faith in Christ? We need in the beginning to sharpen our understanding of what such faith really is. It is certainly more than mental assent to a theory about who Jesus was and did, no matter how orthodox and correct according to historical traditions. As we have said, any faith is a stance or approach to life; that is, an affirmation about the nature of reality and the trust or "ultimate concern" that acts on that affirmation. Faith in Christ, therefore, is the stance that says: We believe we understand something about who Jesus was and what he did; this understanding gives us the key to who we are—a key to the meaning of all life and to the nature of reality itself. And on this assumption we are willing to act, no matter what it costs—that is, to wager or risk our lives upon it. The profession itself is not faith if it is only from the top of our minds while we act upon some other assumption. That assumption, whatever it is, and however unrecognized in the unconscious mind, is our faith.

"Faith is an affirmation and an act that bids eternal truth be

19

present fact." Or it may be an affirmation and an act that attempts to make a false assumption be a present fact and gets hurt badly in the attempt! How do we know an affirmation rests on a sound basis of "eternal truth"? We know by the results in life in the same manner in which any other kind of truth is tested. If our ultimate concern results in negative, hurtful attitudes and acts that impair our ability to live at our best and destroys the healthy relationships needed for the well-being of home, community, and society at large, then I may conclude that there is something wrong with the stance upon which the ultimate concern is expressed. I may be sure that the affirmation is not truth, but rests on shaky foundations. Or to put it in different words, our concern which we make ultimate is based on something which is less than ultimate.

Admittedly when we begin to speak of "ultimates" we are in the realm of value judgments. What may be ultimate for you, may be penultimate to me, and vice versa. And yet, since we have to choose our stance and use our most intelligent understanding based on the evidences available, it is appropriate that we look for the difference faith in Christ makes in contrast with the other faiths.

Suppose I take the stance of faith that says there is a living God in and through and underneath all this mysterious universe, that this God is more than Cosmic Force or Integrating Principle but is also the Source of all Being. A clue to his true nature has been revealed in the finest human spirits of all the ages, including the Buddha, Socrates, and other noble persons; but the fullest, highest clue to the nature of this ground and source of all Being is supremely in the Spirit we call Christ, who was known first and most triumphantly in the life and

20

mighty acts of Jesus of Nazareth and subsequently in the lives and acts of those who have truly followed him.

All right, you say, suppose I take this faith as my stance and act upon it, am willing to stake my life upon it—what difference will it make in finding this precious knowledge of myself?

With this stance I am able to use the good in all the other methods of self-knowledge; but I have much more: I have a vantage point from which right thinking, right meditation, right praying, and right acting are not only more likely, but more effective, so that I will be able to surrender not only my ignorance but my will to ignorance!

To illustrate the value of this vantage point, let us consider the story told by Jesus which is often thought of as the parable of the Prodigal Son, but which Helmut Thielicke has so aptly called the story of the Waiting Father. In it Jesus shows us three important things: (a) why it is so difficult to discover who we are; (b) the results of living in the pigpen of human absurdity; and (c) most important of all, how we can discover who we are—the glorious possibilities of seeing ourselves in the light of reality as revealed in all that we mean when we say "in Christ."

THE DIFFICULTY IN DISCOVERING MY TRUE IDENTITY

The story is contemporary, for it is my story and yours, the story of all mankind. Jesus said this boy came to his father with the request, "Father, give me my share of the property!" (Luke 15:11, NEB). Now to a headstrong young man this seems a reasonable request. So it seems to many of us, and this is the stance we often take toward life:

21

"Give me my share of the property of life and let me do with it as I please!"

Here, Jesus, the Buddha, and modern psychologists agree: *Our ignorance of ourselves is due not so much to the fact that we are holding on to material things and physical pleasures but that we cling to our preconceived ideas about ourselves*, to dreams and longings we have been building up since childhood, caused by our reaction to the humiliating, disappointing, or pleasurable experiences we have known. Like the boy in the story, we hold so tightly to these pictures of ourselves, rooted in the depths of our subconscious minds, that we may not be able to see the true picture. As a result we lose our true selves. Jesus put it succinctly in the great paradox, "He who seeks to save himself [his self-image or picture] shall lose himself; but he who loses [surrenders, denies] himself [his inadequate self-image] shall find himself [who he really is]" (paraphrase of Mark 8:35).

Here is a boy whose sister or whose friend says to him, "You can't sing." He accepts their verdict and he cannot sing. But any voice teacher knows this is not the true fact. Any person can learn to sing a little.

Or perhaps parents or teacher say, "You are dumb in math," and I accept their verdict and live in this grave of a false idea of myself.

Or perhaps I take the opposite reaction: As a child I've been mistreated and made to feel insignificant; so I grow up dreaming of the time when I will come back and "show 'em." So often much of our purpose in life seems to be to "show 'em."

Or perhaps I was poor as a child, so I grow up as the character in Robert Ruark's novel, *Poor No More*,[2] determining that I'm not going to be poor any more.

But whatever my reaction, whether resignation or rebellion, I fail to discover the real me. The true me is lost. I go out like Don Quixote, even with perfectly good personal and social ideals, fighting windmills with my little sword. Finding myself broken and frustrated, I am overwhelmed by life's absurdities. "Give me my share of the property of life," I say, and I miss the share of real values, the true property of life!

Meister Eckhart of the Middle Ages describes our frustration, "A man has as many skins in himself, covering the depths of his heart. Man knows so many other things, he does not know himself. Why thirty or forty skins or hides, just like a bear's, so thick and hard, cover the soul."

What are these skins that hide our real selves? Call it immaturity, or sin, or whatever you will, the proud possessiveness that desperately holds on to false or inadequate self-pictures keeps us ignorant and frustrated.

THE PIGPEN OF ABSURDITY

The story of the Prodigal Son (or the Waiting Father) also tells us the results of not knowing who we are. Jesus said the boy found himself in the pigpen eating the husks that even the pigs had a hard time eating; that is, *having lost our true identity, we lose even the pleasures and security we seek to find.*

All of us have been in that absurd pigpen. Some who read this are there right now: in the pigpen of abnormal anxiety, self-consciousness, costly resentment, and hate. How often even the man whose intelligence is the keenest finds himself like this boy wasting his life substance, if not in riotous living, at least in anxious, resentful living. Every one of us has squandered so much of his time and energy trying to prove something that really does not need proving, to get attention, recognition, or at least security, only to find himself more insecure than ever.

When I say, "Give me my share of the property of life," I may mean the right to indulge my appetite for sex, or food, or liquor, or excitement, or just to be at the top of my profession or business. What's wrong with wanting to be at the top? Nothing at all, except I may have a rigid picture of what it means to be at the top which may become a ceiling to fall down on me. Obviously here is the principal reason not only for sexual offenses and delinquencies, but for so many failures in business or life or in marriage.

"He had spent it all . . . and he began to feel the pinch" (Luke 15:14, NEB). Certainly all of us have felt the pinch of inadequacy and frustration. We are conscious of the absurdity of knowing that we ought to be strong, wise, and sufficient, but we are not. The very moments when we ought to be at our best we often are at our worst. We open our mouths and put our feet in them. In so many ways we begin to feel the pinch!

"Whoever knows the all, but fails to know himself, lacks everything." Thus Jesus is supposed to have said in the Gospel of Thomas (found in an old scroll in an earthen jar in Egypt in 1945). It is certainly true that "if you do not have this self-knowledge within you, what you do have will kill you."

So this boy got to the point of longing to stuff himself with the food that the pigs were eating. We may or may not stuff ourselves with alcohol, or dope, but we may try money, food, or adulation. If a caricature were to be drawn of the average

24

freshman in college or the woman in her club or the business or professional man at his door, it would be of a big shaggy dog, wagging his tail, waiting for someone to pat him on the head! Stuff the pigs are eating! But we eat it up, since there is nothing better. We try to live on that which never satisfies, but we use it to keep from knowing who we really are.

In the comic strip, *Peanuts*, one day Lucy said to Charlie Brown, "All right, you know what I think of world problems? I'll tell you! I'll give them just twelve years to get things straightened out! I want everything settled by the time I'm eighteen! I want to live my adult life in a perfect world! So they better get going!"

The next frame shows Charlie Brown saying to himself, "Now there's an ultimatum to end all ultimatums."

But next morning the strip shows Lucy extending the time a little. "I'll give them twenty years to get things right."

"But suppose they don't?" asks Charlie.

"I'll not give them a second warning!"

Yes, give me my share of the property of life! I demand the world to be the way I want it to be, and they'd better get going! But when eighteen or twenty or forty years are up and the world is not a perfect world, the injustices and inadequacies are still there, my circumstances and position in life are not what I expect. I am bitter, resentful, fed up. I rebel. I may go berserk and become a criminal. Or I may dignify my rebellion and become a Marxist or a revolutionary. Or I may stay with the boredom and meaninglessness and fight it to my dying day, wasting my substance in resentful, anxious living! But either way I take, having missed the vantage point that would help me discover my true self, I never get around to making the fine contribution I could have made to a world on fire. I am lost in the pigpen of absurdity!

AND HE CAME TO HIMSELF

But how do I know who I really am, so that I can accept and become my authentic self and thus make my contribution to this imperfect and absurd old world? Jesus said that this boy at last "came to his senses," "he came to himself." How? In the same way you and I may, by seeing himself in the light of reality, the way things really are: the truth! This is that about which religion and science are both concerned, for truth is one. Physical science deals with one kind of reality and religion and the social sciences with another, but they are not contradictory or mutually exclusive.

But what is reality? That is the heart of the matter. Buddhism and the Eastern religions say that reality is that which is beyond the vicious circle of struggle, suffering, and trouble. To find reality, one disciplines his thoughts and desires so that he gets out of this vicious circle with its chain of reincarnations and ceases to exist as a person. The goal is at last to be lost in the thoughtless, desireless, nothingness of Nirvana! This is surely no vantage point to discover my true self, but rather to lose all self-consciousness and individuality. Also, only a few can reach Nirvana. The remainder are forever doomed to the absurd rat race of desire, suffering, and perpetual reincarnation.

What about the stance of the pseudoscientific mind that sees reality as nothing but a vast impersonal unconscious force, with a set of natural laws that somehow started rolling, we don't know how, or why? All we know is that life is here and there is no discernible purpose or meaning to it all! What contribution does this stance have to make in helping me discover who I am? Well, if I am nothing but "an itch on the epidermis of one of the meanest planets," no wonder I want to scratch! I have not just the "seven-year-itch," but a forty- or eighty-year itch! No wonder believing this I feel myself insignificant and lose myself in the anonymity of the mass. Unless I rebel and become a revolutionary, I am nothing but a cog in an economic machine, a social security number. And even if I rebel, I am still a cog in a party or a state. I have lost my identity.

We can understand the experience of some boys on Parris Island, South Carolina, being turned into U.S. Marines. They had been stripped of their clothes. They were given Marine hair cuts and told to sit on the floor in a little room until they were called for. There they sat, their bodies blue with cold, their heads bald. Shivering, one of them leaned over and whispered to the other, "Who'd you used to be?" No, it isn't funny! It's tragic—the absurdity of the lost identity so familiar today.

But suppose I take the stance of faith in the reality shining in the face of Jesus Christ? I confront the great Spirit at the heart of all things that puts purpose, meaning, and value into life. Reality, says Jesus by his teachings and his life and death, is like the Waiting Father in the story, except he does more than wait for the return of the lost boy. He goes into the very valley of death himself, bearing the sins and sufferings and sorrows of his brethren; and as he does, a light shines into the face of the Waiting Father who shares these sins and sorrows with all of his sons. If this is what God thinks of us, then we ought to think highly of ourselves. If we are "sons," "children of God," then "it doth not yet appear what we shall be." "As

27

many as received him, to them gave he power to become the sons of God" (John 1:12; I John 3:2, KJV).

According to this Christian stance, the only way you and I will ever really see ourselves as we are and are meant to be is here in the light of the reality of the love of God as revealed in Christ—the Christ who is supremely revealed in Jesus of Nazareth and in countless others through the centuries. For in this light we believe that we are created free to become our true selves, to develop and use this mighty universe for the good of all; or, if we choose, to rebel and try to play God and thus inevitably destroy our true identity and destiny. Our great hope and promise is that in the light of his reality we see ourselves as God sees us.

"Impossible!" you say. "How can I know the way God sees me? Besides this is taking a lot for granted, isn't it, that God is in some way personal? How do I know all these things?" These are honest questions deserving honest answers. Certainly the picture of the Waiting Father is anthropomorphic—that is, it pictures God in human terms. And yet, what other choices do we have? If we do not think in *human* terms we must think in *inhuman materialistic* terms. The Waiting Father and the Son returning loved and accepted of course are symbols. Which vantage point will give us the most truthful understanding of ourselves: the vantage point of a vast unconscious force, or of a Waiting Father? To use the latter means at least this much—that we believe we are in some way related to the great Mind and Spirit that brings order and meaning in all this vast universe.

To have faith in the God of Christ does not mean an attempt to confine God to the narrow confines of man, even as

28

noble a man as Jesus; but to believe that the infinite reality is like that: that is, it does not contradict the meaning revealed in Jesus. God is infinitely more, but at least he is as good as the Waiting Father! What I am in his sight, I am no more and no less!

We must first, like this boy, see ourselves as we are compared to what we could be. "How many of my father's paid servants have more food than they can eat, and here am I, starving to death!" (Luke 15:17, NEB.)

This necessity is present in the world of physical becoming. A story in the newspapers recounts the fact that a man of seventy-three died while running a cross-country race in New England. But what was such an old man doing running a race at that age? we may ask. Well, he had been doing it all his life and had won many races. Back when he was a boy, he was a sickly little runt, afflicted with what they called a weak heart. No one would have thought he could be anything much physically. And yet he saw who he really was physically, and through good exercise, good food, he became a physical giant. If this is true physically, how much more mentally and spiritually?

A good illustration of the vantage point one with faith in God possesses is the story of Louis Pasteur, to whom many of us owe perhaps our lives through such discoveries as inoculation and pasteurization. But first he had to "come to himself." As a lad, he was not a brilliant student. He was certainly not a genius. He was a plodder. In school he was made to feel insignificant by the bright boys. He was born into a poor family. He was small of stature. At fourteen he went away to school and failed and came home miserably defeated. But through the encouragement of an old headmaster and a teacher of philosophy, he learned how to be himself, to rise above his fears, and to be saved from his false self-image, which could have been his grave forever. He wanted to enter the Ecole Normale but was afraid he would fail. Then he began to prepare himself spiritually to live. He would go into the church and read by the hour, such a book as that by Joseph Droz, *On Developing Inner Strength*. He found that inner strength through prayer and meditation, through seeing himself as the God of Christ saw him. He learned the truth of the words of the medieval Christian, "What a man is in God's sight, that he is no more and no less!"

He took the competitive exams and failed. He worked harder another year, took them again and won. He began his life's work and became one of the great scientists of all times. But first he had to come to himself. He learned to accept his slow mind, to use his talents to the full, to accept friendship and the encouragement of those who believed in him. He learned to be grateful and generous and to keep steady when under attack. But behind it all was his acceptance of the love and peace of God by which he also accepted his imperfections and conquered even the absurdity of death with its fears! Only thus did he become this great scientist who has so blessed mankind.

Here is the place to begin. To say with Louis Pasteur and the son in the far country, "I will be my authentic self, not as others picture me, or as I desire to be, but as God sees me to be. I will arise and go to my Father. I will stand in the presence of the Highest Reality, not the lowest, or the second best, or the smallest, but the highest!"

What a relief from the laughable and yet tragic human absurdities this viewpoint brings! For the folly of trying to be what we are not is more and more apparent. Then we no longer seek to measure ourselves by others or by ourselves. "What fools they are," wrote Paul, "to measure themselves by themselves to find in themselves their own standard of comparison!" (II Cor. 10:12-13, NEB.) For we know that each one is different, a precious individual in the sight of God—the realistic meaning to our dream of "all men equal." "With us" Paul continues, "there will be no attempt to boast beyond our proper sphere; and our sphere is determined by the limit God laid down for us." But that limit or sphere is much more wonderful than we think. Most of us, say the psychologists, never realize more than 1/20th of our potential. What happens to the 19/20ths? Lost in the pigpen of absurd self-preoccupation seeking to measure ourselves by ourselves or by others.

In a novel by William Saroyan, a teacher of ancient history said to young Homer, who had spoken derisively of his friend Hubert, as one who "seems to think he is better than the other boys":

Yes . . . I know how you feel, but every man in the world *is* better than someone else, and not as good as someone *else*. . . . In a democratic state every man is the equal of every other man up to the point of exertion, and after that every man is free to exert himself to do good or not, to grow nobly or foolishly, as he wishes. . . . If the children of my classroom are human, I do not want them to be alike in their manner of being human. If they are not corrupt, it does not matter to me how they differ from one another. I want each of my children to be himself. . . . I want my children to be *people*—each one separate—each one special—each one a pleasant and exciting variation of all the others.[3]

31

This is the real summit of life. To be what you really are is true joy and freedom. To do this we measure ourselves up to our limits as God knows them and not by the limits of others. How wonderful is the freedom to be my authentic or real self, to escape both the prison house of my own dreams and false self-demands and the prison house of what others would make me. As Robert Browning put it in "Rabbi Ben Ezra":

> All I could never be,
> All, men ignored in me,
> This, was I worth to God, whose wheel the pitcher shaped!"

You and I have to see ourselves in the light of the truth— the Eternal Father as seen in Christ! When we do, notice what happens. The father in Jesus' story went out and put his arms around the boy and a ring on his finger and shoes on his feet.

"Hurry!" he cried. "Let's have a celebration, for this is my son. I thought he was dead but he is alive. He was lost, but now he is found!"

What a celebration indeed when I begin to come to myself—a celebration for me, my family, my world!—when my rebellion is transformed into positive creative channels so that I can be a mediating, a reconciling, rather than a destroying force!

How does it come? Only through what Christians call prayer and worship—right thinking, right meditation—all in the presence of and confronting this Father-like reality. Christian prayer is the conscious turning in thankfulness and intelligent humility to the one who knows who I am and can be, who will forgive me for my past failures and help me in the present to be at my best for my own sake, and for the sake of mankind, and, greatest of miracles—for his sake. His name is Love, his nature is compassion, his will is truth and perfect freedom. For this is not a one-way quest. It is a "double search." It is not so much a matter of finding out who I am as being found!

When I am found by him, it becomes possible for me to say "no" to the imagined self which is either my goal or my limit—and one is as bad as the other. Then I can say "no" to the little self that insists on certain things in order to be happy:

that I must not suffer or see anyone else suffer;

that I must live in a world without trouble and pain for myself and others;

that I must keep my life as it is without changing it;

and that I cannot stand to think of death!

When he finds me I can say "no" to all of these and all other false self-pictures that block my path to knowledge and life.

Then I will be able to say "yes" to the true self, and "yes" to the Waiting Father: "Here I am, make me what I am meant to be . . . even your servant . . . . I would rather be your servant than a slave to my little ego-god! Regardless of what others think, say, or do, let me be and do what is my highest truth!"

Such openness and willingness is mine when I am found by him! I still have a long way to go before realizing my authentic self to the full, but I am on the way!

This is the call that comes to each of us. We are God's sons, whatever that means, and we know only a small part of it now; but we believe it is the symbol of a priceless fact. We are God's sons: Therefore let us live with this absurd faith that turns out to be the only way out of absurdity!

DOING what COMES
NATURALLY

Living by faith in the God of Christ is completely absurd, so say many today. It is absurd to cast your life out upon a noble wager, the end of which you cannot prove by your senses or measure by the exact sciences.

All of us, children of a scientific age, can at least understand such feelings, and, if we are honest, admit we have felt the same way many times. And yet, is it not even more absurd to cast your life out upon the ignoble assumption that human life can be measured entirely by the senses and limited by the exact sciences?

Since both ideas seem absurd, we must choose which absurdity to base our lives upon. Either way, we act on faith as our stance, our ultimate concern, whether we call it that or not. We cannot avoid living by faith, no matter how determined we are to live by sight or the other senses and by logical reasoning. We must decide. Either life has meaning, purpose, value, and direction inherent in the very nature of reality or it doesn't. Either we find that purpose, value, meaning, and direction or we do not. This is not an academic or speculative question but rather a life decision. Whether or not we think it through intellectually, our lives will decide one way or another. Common sense dictates that we consider which way is the most natural—which way in the long run is not absurdity but the deepest realism—and bet our lives on that!

A Broadway musical of several years ago, *Annie Get Your Gun*, describes one approach to the absurdities of existence. It is a simple answer summarized in the title of the song made popular by Ethel Merman, who played the part of Annie Oakley, a vital, lovable young woman in the Wild West. Annie boasted that she could outshoot, outsing, and outdraw any half-dozen mere men. Her favorite song was "Doing What Comes Naturally." By this she meant running, shooting, riding, eating, sleeping, loving.

Who is the truly natural man and when could it be said that we are really doing what comes naturally? Obviously, we will have to go deeper than Annie's definition.

IS THE ANIMAL MAN THE NATURAL MAN?

There are plenty of witnesses to say, no, the truly natural man is more than the healthy animal Annie seems to take for granted.

True, a whole school of popular psychologists gives Annie's answer its backing. We are primarily higher animals, they say; therefore doing what comes naturally is expressing our animal desires in every way as fully as possible. To inhibit these natural desires is to become sick. To express ourselves completely is to be well. Inhibition is the only evil. Self-expression is the supreme good. Ernest Hemingway was fond of saying, "What is moral is what you feel good after, and what is immoral is what you feel bad after." Anything that gives pleasure is good. Now if your animal-like desires run counter to the mores and customs of your society, you may do one of three things: (a) go ahead and defy the customs and do it anyhow; (b) change the mores, if possible; (c) if not and it is too costly to defy them, then adjust to them.

Now, no one can deny that we do have animal desires and functions, but with what a difference! So far as I know, no dog ever committed suicide, no animal ever locked another animal up in a gas furnace and incinerated him. No monkey ever sent another monkey up in a rocket toward the moon, and never will.

Mark Twain, in one of his humorous philosophical sketches entitled "The Damned Human Race," says that he believes in *devolution* rather than *evolution*; that is, man didn't *ascend* from the animals, but rather *descended*. And he makes a strong case:

The higher animals engage in individual fights, but never in organized masses. Man is the only animal that deals in that atrocity of atrocities, War. He is the only one that gathers his brethren about him to go forth in cold blood and with pulse calm to exterminate his kind. . . . Man is the only Slave. And he is the only animal who enslaves. He has always been a slave in one form or another, and has always held other slaves in bondage under him in one way or another. . . . Man is the only Patriot. He sets himself apart in his own country, under his own flag, and sneers at the other nations. . . . And in the intervals between campaigns he washes the blood off his hands and works for "the universal brotherhood of man"—with his mouth. Man is the Religious Animal. . . . He is the only animal that has the True Religion—several of them. He is the only animal that loves his neighbor as himself, and cuts his throat if his theology isn't straight.[1]

There is too much truth for comfort in these satirical words of Mark Twain. Yes, this is the absurdity of human life: We too belong to this "damned human race." As long as we hold to a rigid picture of ourselves and what we demand in order to be happy, as long as we set ourselves up as little kings or gods, determined to make our own heaven, we always end up by creating our own hell of isolation, hostility, loneliness, and death. Yes, this "damned" pride and the resulting loneliness are different from the experience that any mere animal can know. If we are ruled by our egos so that each of us tries to be king and make others our subjects, then of course we will have to fight it out until one or the other abdicates his kingship, and peace is possible only through a truce between wars.

Mark Twain's satire is indeed one side of the truth. But there is another side: the infinite possibilities of human creativity and harmony which, when we lose them, simply add to the tragedy and absurdity. For God is not to blame for our human evil. To rebel at creation and the Creator because of these contradictions is to lose the whole point of the Hebrew-Christian faith. This point of hope and meaning declares our human freedom: We are free to act like egoistic kings if we choose and thereby to be scattered and destroyed by our pride. But we are also free to accept ourselves as loved by God—gathered in love and humility, children and brothers in the family of God, the Lord of the Universe—and to find the peace and joy of unlimited growth for which we were intended.

Recall the story of the first scattering, the fratricidal hate of Cain who killed his brother Abel before the very altar where they were supposed to be worshiping God! Cain was driven out from his brethren, not by God, but by his own rebellious hatred. In this sense, therefore, God does not punish us for our sins; he lets us punish ourselves. We are all, to the extent that we rebel and miss the freedom to love and work together in peace and harmony, sons and daughters of Cain!

We are free to choose which side of the truth of human nature to bet our lives upon. We may pick the animal side of man, but we need to hear the warning of George Bernard Shaw:

Man is the only animal of which I am thoroughly and cravenly afraid. I never thought much of the courage of the lion tamer, for inside the cage he is at least safe from other men. There is less harm in a well-fed lion. He has no ideals, no sex, no parties, no nation, no class, in short, no reason to destroy anything that he doesn't want to eat.[2]

"To say that men behave like beasts is always unfair to the beasts!"[3]

Yes, we are animal, but so much more. We may do much that animals are utterly incapable of doing, both good and bad. We may rise to godlike heights or sink to abysmal depths. Two healthy animals can cohabit harmoniously, but not always we human beings. A dozen things can mar our physical harmony. Animals have sex relations, but no animal could have expressed the love described in Elizabeth Barrett Browning's *Sonnets from the Portuguese,* nor painted Millet's "Angelus," nor written Brahms' *Symphony No. 1 in C Minor!*

Pierre Lecomte du Nuöy's *Human Destiny* is a remarkably vivid description of the conviction of a great biologist that evolution alone cannot account for the idea of God in human life and the spiritual longings that cause us to sacrifice ourselves for others. Something more is required, he believes, than causal mechanistic evolution where the mutations come by chance.

Many present-day biologists and anthropologists are emphasizing the discontinuity as well as the continuity in evolution. Contrary to Darwin's confident declaration in *Origin of the Species* that natural selection could never advance through sudden leaps, but must take place in short and sure but slow steps, they are just as confidently convinced of sudden leaps— unusual mutations—as part of the evolutionary process. The emphasis is on indeterminancy and unpredictability. Pierre Teilhard de Chardin, the Jesuit scientist, sees "great leaps of discontinuity" such as the jump from 300 cc to 1500 cc brain capacity in the skulls of prehistoric man. He speaks of this as the *"Birth of Thought"* in "the age of the mind." [4] To explain this by chance is the height of absurdity. A far more rational postulate is to believe that God is still creating the universe and man.

Lecomte du Nuöy declares that in spite of "an immense number of facts which for more than a thousand million years have tended to assure the persistence of the species . . . all of a sudden we are confronted with tendencies leading exactly in the opposite direction." Then Something Beyond began saying to our humankind,

So far thou wast only concerned with living and procreating; thou couldst kill, steal food or mates, and go to sleep peacefully after having obeyed all the instincts put in thee to assure a numerous descendance. From this day on, thou shalt combat these instincts, thou shalt not kill, thou shalt not steal, thou shalt not covet. Thou shalt only sleep peacefully if thou hast mastered thyself. Thou shalt be ready to suffer and to give thy life, which yesterday thou wast forced to defend at any price. . . . To live, eat, fight, and procreate are no longer thy principal aims. Death, hunger, slavery and chastity endured for a high ideal are nobler ends. And thou must be noble. It is the will of the new being who has risen in thee and whom thou must accept as master even though he curbs thy desires. . . . Alas, this new being does not yet inhabit all hearts. . . .[5]

Surely this last sentence is the understatement of the age. And yet the presence of such new beings is our greatest hope—the fact that there are in every age "new creations in Christ," as Paul calls them, who have used their animal desires and instincts to beautify and enlarge their lives and the lives of others rather than to make ugly and to destroy—this is our hope as the foretaste of what human nature really is and can become.

Our Hebrew-Christian faith at its best is not a denial but an affirmation of life, not only of some vaguely spiritual life but of the physical as well. It declares that sex is holy, the body is good when treated with reverence and respect!

"Know you not that your body is the temple of the Holy Spirit . . . so glorify God in your body!" (I Cor. 6:19-20, italics added.)

The asceticism of much so-called Christian faith which thinks of the body as evil and the physical, animal desires as our enemies is a perversion of this main line conviction of the Hebrews carried over into the New Testament: "So God created man in his own image, in the image of God he created him; male and female he created them. . . . And God saw everything that he had made, and behold, it was very good!" (Gen. 1:27, 31.)

THE TRULY HUMAN IS THE NEW BEING IN CHRIST!

Thus the Apostle Paul affirms to the Corinthians:

[As new beings in Christ] we have received not the spirit of the world, but the Spirit which is from God. . . . The unspiritual man does not receive the gifts of the Spirit of God, for they are folly to him, and he is not able to understand them because they are spiritually discerned (1 Cor. 2:12, 14).

That is, there are just two kinds of men: those who have more and more of the mind of Christ and those who do not. To make such a statement may seem dogmatic and arbitrary at first. Before we shrug it off, however, let us examine the meaning of "the mind of Christ," which is obviously a symbol representing what as Christians we believe is most real in our human life. This can best be done by an existential examination of two kinds of persons, which for the time being we will designate as those having the mind and spirit of Christ and those who do not.

The man without the mind and spirit of Christ is the subhuman, subnatural man. He is really doing what comes unnaturally, because he loses his highest possibilities. He is "dead through the trespasses and sins" (Eph. 2:1). Here are two old words whose meaning is lost to most modern people and need

41

to be translated. The Greek word we translate "sin" comes from the sport of archery and means "missing the mark." The word for "trespasses" means literally "to slip or fall." The man who uses only his human, animal faculties without having his mind and reason inspired by the Spirit always fails to be what he can and ought to be and do. He misses the mark. He who is "unspiritual" always slips or falls from his high estate, his true possibilities.

Now, no bird ever misses his mark. A carrier pigeon was released by some arctic explorers and flew several thousand miles straight to its home with the message tied to its leg. The pigeon did not miss the mark. A dog is a dog, nothing more nor less. He always acts like a dog with canine consistency and dignity; but a man has to become a man. As Joseph Haroutunian, a professor of systematic theology at the Divinity School of the University of Chicago, said, "Manhood is a responsibility to become . . . Human nature is not something with which we are born, a fact, like a stone or an animal. To be human is to struggle to maintain the becoming of a man . . . Forever do we need to be working to prevent being dehumanized."

Walt Whitman said that a cow never lies awake at night to weep over its sins. No, but we do, because we are endowed with infinite capacities beyond those of a cow.

Jack London once wrote a detective story entitled, "Just Meat." It is the story of two robbers who burglarized the home of a rich man. During a struggle they shot the man, and as he lay dying on his living room floor, one of the robbers said to the other, "I'm sorry we had to kill him; we only meant to rob him." To which the other robber replied, "Why worry, he was just meat!" As they separated, each going a different way

42

to the designated hideout, one robber got some coffee while the other picked up some steaks for food. In order to get all the loot, each robber poisoned the other's food. The donor of the coffee drank no poisoned coffee, and the donor of the steaks ate no poisoned steaks, but each poisoned the other, crying, "Just meat!"

Without what we are calling "the mind of Christ" we lose our humanity and are "just meat." As the subhuman, subnatural man who refuses my relationship with the Spirit, I am never able to fulfill my true destiny. As such I kill my ideals and longings for the highest. The trouble is that they won't stay dead. They come up in the most unexpected and disconcerting places: in anxiety, in dejection, in frustration, and in boredom and resulting destructiveness.

Boredom is indeed the most deadly disease of our times. Society is now one horde of people formed into "two mighty tribes, the bores and the bored." Indeed we are miserable without fulfilling our true spiritual natures. We can never rest content, for like a fish out of water we have lost our native habitat. We can sympathize with Lord Illingworth in Oscar Wilde's *A Woman of No Importance* when Gerald, the young hopeful said, "I suppose society is wonderfully delightful!"

The old society lion answered with a shrug, "To be in it is merely a bore. But to be out of it simply a tragedy." [6]

With boredom and anxiety of meaninglessness go self-disgust, lovelessness, and hate.

> A cheerful old bear at the zoo
> Could always find something to do.
> When it bored him, you know,

To walk to and fro,
He reversed it and walked fro and to! [7]

But we are not cheerful old bears and we cannot overcome
our boredom and anxiety by abandoning ourselves, as
Nietzsche, Comte, and their modern counterparts, the logical
positivists, would have us do, to a devoted allegiance to world-
liness. I may try it, as a majority of Westerners are trying. But
see what happens: If there is no higher destiny or value than
that found within myself, then I must make my own laws. If
there are no moral and spiritual laws in the very nature of
things, if God is dead, then I must accept all the drives, demands, urges, itches "with magnificent consent." For a while
I enjoy the playboy philosophy, "Anything that is pleasurable
is good," but someway I must learn how to accept the un-
acceptable conflicts between these demands together with the
absurdities of my imperfections and sufferings and those of my
fellows. For now the only wrong I can do is to wish to be other
than I am, namely, a little finite creature alone in a friendless
universe. To be able to do this requires some doing indeed!
To be joyous and strong as the conflicts deepen and the frailties
and yawning abyss of human decay confront me—to be joyous,
wise and happy in it all—requires me to be a superman. But
always on the superman falls the shadow:

> Between the desire
> And the spasm
> Between the potency
> And the existence
> Between the essence

44

And the descent
Falls the Shadow

. . . .

This is the way the world ends
Not with a bang but a whimper.[8]

Without "the mind of Christ," at least enough to give meaning and resources to my frail human life, I lose my humanity! This is the witness of human experience in every age.

There is another fact, however you explain it, to which human experience gives continuous witness: The man who has more and more of the mind of Christ is able to live not only in this physical world at his best, finding the fullest enjoyment of material and sensual things; but, what is more difficult, he is the one most able to live in the social and moral world in the truly natural way.

That we have such ability is poetically described by some lines written a few days before his death by John Gillespie Magee, nineteen-year-old ace with the Royal Canadian Air Force:

Oh I have slipped the surly bonds of earth
  And danced the skies on laughter-silvered wings;
Sunward I've climbed, and joined the tumbling mirth
  Of sun-split clouds—and done a hundred things
You have not dreamed of—wheeled and soared and swung
  High in the sunlit silence. Hov'ring there,
I've chased the shouting wind along, and flung
  My eager craft through footless halls of air.

Up, up the long, delirious, burning blue
  I've topped the wind-swept heights with easy grace

Where never lark, or even eagle flew—
And, while with silent lifting mind I've trod
  The high untrespassed sanctity of space,
Put out my hand and touched the face of God.[9]

This is something no animal-man could do—not only the miracle of physical flight, but the greater experience Magee described as "touching the face of God." Contrast these words with those of the Russian astronaut, Titov, who after seventeen orbits a hundred miles above the earth in space, declared with assurance, "There is no God . . . I was up there and didn't see him." Of course he didn't see God with his physical eyes, any more than did John Glenn on his history-making flight into space. But there is a spiritual reality which both John Magee and John Glenn saw which Titov could not see, because "The unspiritual man does not receive the gifts of the Spirit of God, for they are folly to him, and he is not able to understand them because they are spiritually discerned."

In the bitter words of Nickles who played the part of the devil in *J.B.*, the modern counterpart of the book of Job, man is an

Animal like any other
Calculated for the boughs of
Trees and meant to chatter and be grateful!
But womb-worm wonders and grows wings.[10]

Yes, we may be womb-worms, but we also grow wings of wonder and trust, of aspiration, of love and of hope! One of the greatest evidences of the living God and our high destiny is that we who are born in the womb like any animal have within us the power to rise to godlike heights: Christ on the Cross, Socrates drinking the hemlock, Father Damien among the lepers, Albert Schweitzer and Tom Dooley in Africa and Laos, and other great spirits known or unknown to the world. These are among those who to me truly represent the natural man.

HOW DO I KNOW WHICH CHOICE TO MAKE IN ORDER TO DO WHAT COMES NATURALLY?

"A tree is known by its fruit" (Matt. 12:33), said Jesus. It would take a superman indeed to be his own God. Nietzsche and the philosophers who proclaimed the death of God must be prepared to accept the death of man as man also! Nietzsche looked for the coming of such supermen without a conscience, with no demand to their earthly desires. The Nazi regime arose dedicated to the creation of such supermen with the theme song of "Joy, joy, joy!" But history says they methodically created only sub-men with neither conscience nor compassion, neither joy nor peace, neither wisdom nor strength, supermen turned into devils hated by others and in the end, hated by themselves. Such sub-men are found not only in Germany, but in Russia and Cuba and America, and wherever man tries to make himself God. The bitterness and destructiveness of the Nazi, the Communist, the racist, the money- or thing- or sex-centered man, are all unnatural, the denial of our true humanity. The absurdity of our failures to use our spiritual capacities produces the sub-human, sub-animal man whose very existence is a tragedy and a threat to all other existence.

Who is the truly natural man? Judge a tree by its fruits. Is he the man of the world who says now, as men of the world

47

have always said, that to have it in your power to avenge yourself of your enemy and not to do so is a sign of weakness? Or is
Jesus the truly natural man, who said in effect, "Forgive those
who hurt you. Do something positive in return, if possible,
that may restore the relationship between you"?

The man of the world says with Plutarch, "The sign of a
good man is to be useful to his friends and terrible to his
enemies." But Jesus said, "Love your enemies" (Matt. 5:44).

Is the truly natural man the one who says, "Get all you can
and keep all you can for yourself, this is the first law of life"?
Or the one who with Jesus in effect says, "Give and serve all
you can. Life is in giving and not in getting. He who is servant
of the most is the greatest."

Which is the truly natural man: the one who is able thus to
love and serve with a purpose that transcends life's absurdities;
or the self-seeking, unloving man (or woman) who becomes
so self-centered that out of bitterness and boredom he has to
fight and destroy not only others but in the end himself?

Deep in our hearts we know the answer. As we read the
scorching bitter experiences of the past fifty years in human
history we are sure of it:

The only natural man is the one who is able to love wisely
and well.

Not a possessive, desiring love but a strong, wise giving-love
that accepts the facts of human imperfection with its selfishness and evil and sees beneath a deeper set of facts that point
to a new kind of man, what the apostle Paul calls "the new
creation in Christ Jesus." The most natural thing for our human life is not the law that says a man must live, so do anything necessary for your comfort, pleasure, safety, and security.

The highest law is the law of Christ that says a man must be willing to die before he can live. The cross of pain and suffering voluntarily borne when necessary for the sake of others is the only way to life for a person, a family, a nation, a world. And this power to bear the burdens and sufferings of others in wise, patient but strong love comes from the living God!

"You he made alive in Christ!" This is the realistic good news of the New Testament. The spiritual man judges all things, but he himself is judged by no merely sub-natural man. For who knows the mind of the Lord? And who can advise him? The answer is clear. "No one." But, says Paul, "we have the mind of Christ!" That is to say, no one of our finite human minds can encompass and describe the mind of the mighty Lord of the universe. His wisdom and infinitude of purpose cannot be grasped by us except in tiny glimpses. But one of these glimpses—the brightest and fullest by far permitted to man—is in the life and death and victory of the spirit as seen in Jesus whom we call Christ the Lord. The truly natural man possesses the mind of Christ: In him we see a clue to our true selves, to our neighbors, to our own destinies, to the nature of reality, and are able to act accordingly.

If this is true, then we have something that is priceless and that all mankind desperately needs. If untrue, then we will have to "out-Nietzsche" Nietzsche and try our best to make our own laws, guarantee our own security, pump up our own joy, and take whatever beauty is left in the ashes of despair.

How will we know? Only by the acid test of experience: the experience of the past which the wise may read and the experience of the present which the wise use to test the answer of the past. In any case there is no proof except in the living.

One cannot say intelligently whether or not the mind of Christ is the natural or the unnatural way of life until he has committed himself to discover and live by this mind. Experience is indeed the acid test of any faith.

HOW DOES ONE GET THE MIND OF CHRIST?

Let us go a bit further in the meaning of faith in Jesus Christ as Lord. The phrase, "Jesus Christ is Lord," was the earliest summary of the Christian faith.

Here again we face the use of timeworn symbols whose meaning evades most moderns. Some would abandon the use of the words "Christ is Lord" altogether. But we cannot evade the impact on human life of the event in history seen in the life, death, and resurrection of Jesus. While scholars who search for the most accurate descriptions of the historical Jesus may differ on the exact words he said and the nature of the event, none of us who have met him in the Gospels and in the continuing community of those who seek to be guided by his mind and spirit can evade the sense of reality which confronts us in him.

True, under the superficial banner of Christ untold evils have been perpetrated on mankind from the time of the Crusades and the Inquisitions to the witch-burnings in colonial America and to the witch-hunting in modern America. While many things that have been done in the name of Christ are abhorrent, false and utterly contradictory to the spirit and mind that was in Jesus, we cannot avoid him nor escape him. Let us seek to dig beneath the old words, "Jesus Christ is Lord" and find the eternal meanings that lead us to the truly natural life, "new creations in Christ Jesus."

Millions of Christians today accept "Jesus Christ is Lord" from the top of their minds. The question is: What would be required of me if I accept Jesus Christ as Lord not only from the top but from the bottom of my mind? For the mind of Christ merely as an ideal, a superficial, intellectual assent, is elusive, abstract, worthless, yes, even harmful. For it may give me a false sense of pious security. It may keep me from confronting the realistic demands of the mind of Christ in my daily choices. It is worthless and destructive unless and until it becomes the source of my motives and the direction for my action. Only when I have made him Lord of all my thoughts, desires, and acts will I truly have the mind of Christ.

We know what it means to have the mind of the gutter! It means that we think, talk, and act like those who live in the gutter of vulgarity and self-indulgence. To have the mind of Christ means that we think, talk, and act in the spirit that moved the teachings and acts of Jesus and of those noble souls through the centuries who have followed him, or who, in other ages, have had the same spirit. Emil Brunner wrote,

When this Man confronts us, we know we are confronting One possessing absolute authority . . . not merely His Speech, . . . His word, but to His Person. In Him there meets us one who is "Our Lord," One whom we cannot evade, in whose Presence self-assertion is impossible. . . . He *is* what He preaches and He *preaches* what He himself is: the Presence of God as Lord.[11]

The word "lord" means one who has absolute authority, one whom we obey at all costs. There are two kinds of lords: (a) one who forces us into servitude; and (b) one to whom we give voluntary obedience, "in whose service is perfect freedom." The lordship of Christ is voluntary, out of love and devotion. We are never forced into a commitment. God whom we meet in Christ sets us free to try desperately to keep our little self-made crowns in place. In so doing we often surrender to some little no-god-tyrant who promises to help us keep our crowns. For man will serve God or he will serve a tyrant. This we do: if not the tyrant of communism or some other all-obsessing idea, our own brand of economic materialism—what Vance Packard [12] calls "planned obsolescence," a prosperity in America that is built on planned waste.

If the God of Christ is not our Lord, then our lord may be the Little-Tyrant-of-Things. As one character in Lorraine Hansberry's play, *Raisin in the Sun*, put it: "I want so many things, it drives me crazy!"

Or we may have as lord the Little-Tyrant-of-the-State, an excessive nationalism that is so destructive in our modern world.

Or the Little-Tyrant-of-the-Group: conformism, racism.

Even in the institutional church the "Organization Man" seeks to be our lord.

But down underneath, and making possible all these little tyrannies with their unnatural and devastating effects, is the worst tyrant of all. Rabindranath Tagore, the Indian poet, describes him as one who follows man in arrogance and pride, with a shallow understanding of his own importance—man's "own little self, his Lord."

Surely it is this Little Lord Self that is back of our human perversions and the resulting evils. No one can know the mind of Christ, much less live by it, until he has dealt firmly and realistically with the Little Lord Self. The apostle Paul said with deadly sincerity, "I die daily. . . . I am crucified with Christ: nevertheless I live; yet not I, but Christ liveth in me: and the life which I now live in the flesh I live by the faith of the Son of God, who loved me, and gave himself for me" (I Cor. 15:31; Gal. 2:20, KJV). What did he mean by "dying daily," by being "crucified with Christ"? Something very practical and necessary but very costly for every one of us before he is able to think of being and doing that which is truly natural and right.

There are two parts of a valid faith as we said in the last chapter: An affirmation and an act that bids eternal truth be present fact. First an affirmation as to my ultimate concern— that which I believe is worthy of my ultimate allegiance. I say "Christ is Lord," that is, I affirm that in him is a clue to the eternal mind of God. His Spirit is the truth, that is, the way God and man really are. All the greatest and most natural spirits who ever lived are to some degree like him.

Then must come an act of my total personality, a commitment of my mind, my will, my desires to him, for he is my ultimate concern in all my living. I "crown him lord of all." The Revelation to John symbolically describes the four and twenty elders before the throne, casting their crowns before Christ. In the old days of kings a crown was a symbol of authority. To cast my crown before Christ means that the Little Lord Self abdicates from the throne of my desires and my will. Before I cast my crown before Christ, so that his mind and spirit rule my mind, I must die to the Little Lord Self.

To make clear what this means, let me use a parable. In my college days I played the trumpet in the McMurry College

53

Indian Band. I also enjoyed participating in a small orchestra where the opportunity to play jazz excited me tremendously. Suppose one day I take my trumpet and go to New York City where I sit enthralled as the great master, Arturo Toscanini, directs the N.B.C. Symphony Orchestra. As I listen my mind is captured by the music. I crown Toscanini "Lord of all Music." When the concert is over, I dare to go to the platform and say, "Mr. Toscanini, would you consider taking me as one of your trumpeters—even just as a substitute? Teach me to play in your great orchestra!"

Marvel of marvels, he does. He sits me down, perhaps as fourth or fifth trumpeter. The rehearsal begins. Of course I make mistakes. I play out of time and miss a few notes. He comes over to correct me. This I don't like. He does it a second and third time. Now I say to him, in anger, "Mr. Toscanini, don't you know that I have my own mind about playing a trumpet? Why I knew how to play a trumpet long before I met you! Who are you to tell me how to play?"

With that display of egoism, I find myself outside the concert hall, no longer even a substitute in Toscanini's orchestra. But with a sense of hurt pride and dogged freedom I go to a little night spot in Greenwich Village where I join a jazz orchestra in which I am permitted complete musical self-expression. I play what I want when I want to, and the others have to try to fit in with me. There are a few moments of superficial satisfaction, but I am deeply dissatisfied. I long to make great music.

At last, with real penitence, I go back and fall down at the feet of the master and say, "Mr. Toscanini, will you take me back? I'll listen and learn. I want your mind to teach my mind."

Another miracle! This great man graciously forgives me and takes me back. I surrender my pride and begin to learn. At last comes the hour when I join in making heavenly music in his symphony!

This parable is a pale illustration of what happens when I crown Jesus Christ Lord of All. For he is not only the Lord of beauty and music but the spirit and mind revealed in him is the spirit and mind that rules the universe. Therefore he is the only one who can save me from this proud little Lord Self. Unlike Toscanini who would take me back two or three times, but no more, by his grace Christ has and will take me back hundreds of times. But the principle is the same: Until I come to the place where I am willing to surrender my mind to his, I will never be able to play in his heavenly orchestra in which something of the truth and harmony of eternity begins to be sounded through my little instrument. When I am willing and ready, I am saved by grace and through faith from this little Lord Self, and I am able to live and act more and more according to the mind of Christ.

But before I make the commitment of faith, it is necessary to be confronted by the majesty and beauty of Christ's music, to wait and listen, as the truth is seen and the love is heard from his life and teachings and from the life and ministry of others who reflect his spirit. Only then do I cast my crown before him and find my little self lost in wonder, love, and praise.

"You he made alive . . . in Christ!" (Eph. 2:1.) Then I can be and do that which comes naturally!

O glorious freedom! O magnificent life!
O Light of Christ, shine in the darkness of my mind,
Drive out the pride and vanity, the self-sickness and sorrow.
Let thy mind be in me that by thy Spirit I shall judge all things,
Meet and overcome all things, both now and evermore!

⇄
SET FREE
to CARE

Through science and human ingenuity we have learned to free ourselves from the physical limitations of gravity and space; but we have not yet found the freedom to love in Christlike concern for the highest good of all men as well as for the good of our own family, group, or nation.

This height of absurdity is symbolized by a cartoon of a football team lined up on the field for their first game, black grease around their eyes, battle gear in place, and a look of existential anxiety on their faces. The coach is saying with great urgency, "The first thing I want you to do is to forget the world situation!"

We are all likely to feel as did that coach. Frustrated by the demands upon our consciences of all the injustices and evils in our world of race, war, poverty, starvation, disease, and suffering, we want to get on with our own little game. We deeply desire to bury the world situation and forget it, taking care of our own little needs. And we may succeed for a time, but the absurd loss of our power to love is one of the most costly absurdities of our human drama.

We talk about love, sing about it, worry about it, need it, hunger for it; but when it comes to loving with the strong, wise, responsible caring that is so necessary for the well-being of our persons, our homes, and our world, we are so often unable.

We have material power to burn in the almost unimaginable 1,500,000-pound thrust provided by the Saturn rocket, able to put a 37,700 pound capsule into orbit around the earth. We have prospects of infinitely larger rockets, so that within a few years we expect to send men to the moon and back. Scientists estimate we have had more power available in the last fifteen years than was used in all the previous history of man. Indeed we are free to make the earth a paradise; but we are also free to turn it into a charred ruin in which even the buzzards are either incinerated or poisoned!

Mankind is like the four-year-old boy visiting his father whose job was the operation of a huge bulldozer. The father climbed off the machine and left the motor running. Somehow, the boy slipped away from his dad and climbed onto the mighty bulldozer. He knew how to start it, but he did not know how to stop it. The newspaper account described the wreckage and terror wrought by the ten-ton monster with a four-year-old at the controls. This is a parable of our twentieth century absurdity: Human life is free to control much of the power of the physical universe and yet is unable to control our human passions, hates, prejudices!

The difference a vital faith in God as revealed in Christ

makes is nowhere more evident than at this critical point of human absurdity: Those of us who have more than a superficial assent to Christ, who make his mind and spirit Lord of our lives, are free to love wisely, responsibly, effectively. We possess the priceless gift of strength and power in our inner being—Christ dwelling in our hearts in love! (See Eph. 3:16-17.) To possess this gift in increasing fullness is to be the truly natural man that God intended us to be—the second Adam whose Christlike concern controlling our desires and acts is the one thing that can prevent all that is worthy in life from being crushed and life itself from coming to a sorry end.

Is this a true statement of the facts, or isn't it? Each of us must decide, using the best information and observations at our disposal, but in the end the decision is a faith decision, requiring commitment and action on that commitment.

LIFE WITH AND WITHOUT FAITH

At least it is clear that, without such a faith-stance, our lives are unnatural, subhuman; we are subanimal. We gain some insight into the validity of this faith-stance by observing what happens to human life with and without the mind and spirit of Christlike love.

First, in our personal relationships in the family. No mother dog or bear feeds on her young, but plenty of human mothers, fathers, husbands, and wives do. We often feed our egos at the expense of our children or our mates. We try to find emotional satisfactions from those we love, and often use them as things to satisfy our desires or to make up for our own sense of failure.

Our love may be soft and easy, what has been called

"momism" or "smother love." A mother or father or marriage partner says to the one loved, "See. I sacrifice so much for you. Just look at all I do for you. You would not want to disappoint your own mother. Therefore do as I say." On the other hand, love may be harsh and dominating. Either way, when it is possessive it is hurtful and results in hatred and even destructiveness in the relationship.

Without some fresh and vital power to care responsibly, the love we bear for others becomes disappointing, even ruinous. What we call love is often destructive, as any minister, judge, social worker, or doctor can testify. The bitter refrain of countless persons is, "I want love more than anything in the world; but the more I want it, the less I receive, and the less I am able to give!" [1]

The same absurdity is revealed when we seek to love our fellows on a wider scale. It is natural for the human spirit to react against injustice wherever it is found, especially if related to ourselves. But not exclusively the latter, for there is that in all of us, unless completely killed by years of conditioning, that feels the woes and hurts of our fellowman. This is one of the characteristics that reveals what the Bible speaks of as "the image of God" in every man. But look what happens when we lose faith in God. We rebel at the injustices so obvious in human life. We conclude, with J.B. (in the play portraying a modern Job),

> If God is God He is not good,
> If God is good He is not God.[2]

Therefore there is no God! Since these injustices and absurdities remain, therefore God is either dead or unjust. So we rebel, saying, "Since God will not bring justice, we will make justice ourselves." We set out with great sincerity and devotion to establish justice and right wrongs. In so doing we become little gods ourselves, setting up our own laws of right and wrong, administering punishment, taking justice in our own hands.

Albert Camus' *The Rebel* is the most careful and objective documenting of the results in the lives of those who believe that "God is dead" to be found anywhere in literature. At last, he says, rebellion at God makes the man who once trembled at the suffering of a child rationalize the necessity for murder of countless innocent people, including many children. Speaking of Ivan Karamazov in Dostoevski's *The Brothers Karamazov*, Camus points out that from the moment that he (Ivan) rejects divine coherence and tries to discover his own rule of life, he recognizes the legitimacy of murder. Since there is no Divine Law and all is permitted, Ivan can kill his father or at least allow him to be killed—and condones crime, in principle.[3]

Also, says Camus, when man rebels at God and goes out to make justice as if he were God, he is impatient when he finds that other men don't cooperate with him. They are weak and more interested in pleasures and bread than in freedom and justice. So in order to accomplish his purpose he has to use others, even to enslave them. In this way "the land of humanism has become the Europe of today, the land of inhumanity." [4] Morals without God become demonic. Rebellion at God and love for man leads only to making man God and others his slaves, resulting in more injustice and suffering than ever!

Albert Camus is caught between an honest appreciation of the absurdity of man without God and an acceptance of some divine source of the love which is required to lift man above the destructiveness of his lovelessness and pride. In the last few pages of this remarkable description of the disaster that has come to man because "God is dead," Camus makes the affirmation which is the thesis of this chapter,

Then we understand that rebellion cannot exist without a strange form of love. . . . It is love and fecundity or it is nothing at all. Revolution without honor, calculated revolution which, in preferring an abstract concept of man to a man of flesh and blood [and to a God who cares personally for man], denies existence as many times as is necessary, puts resentment in the place of love. Immediately rebellion, forgetful of its generous origins, allows itself to be contaminated by resentment; it denies life, dashes toward destruction, and raises up the grimacing cohorts of petty rebels, embryo slaves all of them, who end by offering themselves for sale, today, in all marketplaces of Europe, to no matter what form of servitude. It is no longer revolution or rebellion, but rancor, malice, and tyranny.

What then is our hope? Or is there any? Here Camus affirms his faith in the possibilities of human life, which requires something which we Christians call God. Whether or not he uses the word is beside the point. Listen as he confesses his faith:

Then when revolution in the name of power and of history becomes a murderous and immoderate mechanism, a new rebellion is consecrated in the name of moderation and of life. We are at that extremity now. At the end of this tunnel of darkness, however, there is inevitably a light, which we already divine and for which we only have to fight to ensure its coming. All of us, among the ruins, are preparing a renaissance beyond the limits of nihilism. But few of us know it.[5]

THE STRANGE FORM OF LOVE

"Then we understand that rebellion cannot exist without a strange form of love!" What is this strange form of love we need in order to live in the light?

Love can be so many things. The word in English is so inadequate. We may be excused for feeling with Aldous Huxley that

of all the worn, smudged, dog's-eared words in our vocabulary, "love" is surely the grubbiest, smelliest, slimiest. Bawled from a million pulpits, lasciviously crooned through hundreds of millions of loudspeakers, it has become an outrage to good taste and decent feeling, an obscenity which one hates to pronounce. And yet it has to be pronounced, for after all, love is the last word! [6]

Yes, the word "love" in its truest meaning is the last word. The apostle Paul put it so well in the great "Hymn to Love": "If I give away all I have, and if I deliver my body to be burned, but have not love, I gain nothing" (I Cor. 13:3). What is this love that is ours and humanity's greatest need?

It is not merely an affection. We must have something more than a care for cars or cats, an affection for dogs, or even a "neighborly feeling for people." In the comic strip, *Peanuts*, Lucy says to Charlie Brown, "Charlie Brown, you will never make a good doctor, because you don't love mankind." To which Charlie replies, "I do too love mankind. It's people I can't stand!"

Jean-Paul Sartre, in the play *No Exit*, describes the absurdity of three people, one man and two women, who after death find themselves locked up in a well-furnished room with no way to escape each other. They discover that "Hell is other people."

Until we escape the Little Lord Self that expects to be served, worshiped, idolized, pleased, of course we are in hell; for hell is other people who get in our way!

Hence such an affectionate feeling for people is good and fine, so far as it goes; but it may be pure sentimentality which evaporates when we need love most. Napoleon was said to have had an involuntary kindness at times. Once on an Italian battlefield he saw a dog howling over the dead body of its master. Later he described his feelings:

> The poor beast seemed to be asking for an avenger, or begging help. I was profoundly moved by the dog's suffering, and at that moment I should have been very much in the mood to grant quarter to an enemy. . . . Such is man; so little can he count upon his moods. Impassively I had sent my soldiers into the battle; dry-eyed I had watched them marching past in an advance where thousands of them would meet their fate; then I was shaken to the depths by the howling of a dog.[7]

His sentimental love for a dog did not prevent him from being one of the most cruel men of history. Love as sentimental affection is not enough to change a Napoleon or anyone else into a being who cares responsibly for others.

Love must also be something more than friendship, as important and beautiful as that is. I have led several "goodwill tours" seeking to make friends in many lands. I believe in cultivating friendships with other people, including my wife. One ought to be friends with one's marriage partner. But this is not enough. For to be a friend means you find one who agrees with you in some important interests, such as hunting, fishing, hi-fi and stereo, or what have you. And if we get to know people of different races and nations we will find such friendship of common interests. But what about the times when we disagree—even in the family—and violently? Speaking of the love even for enemies as described by Jesus in the Sermon on the Mount, James Moffatt said, "To 'love' them [the enemies] does not mean that we are pleased with them in their present position, or that we are to be amiable to them; it means a new moral relationship, for which 'love' was a new term." [8]

This love we need must not only be more than friendship and affection. It must also be more than love as "eros," the possessing, desiring, sometimes romantic love that sees in others something attractive, desirable, worthy of our appreciation. For there are always, even in our mates, some things that are not desirable, not worthy, and even things despicable. While romantic, eros love, or even appreciative love is beautiful indeed, it certainly is not the cement that can hold our homes together, much less this maddened and selfish old world.

William Morris wrote a poem entitled, "Love Is Enough." Someone wrote a brief review of it in two words: "It isn't." [9] Certainly love as affection, friendship, eros—"need love," "desiring love"—is not enough. For we have always had an abundance of these so-called natural loves. Our human situation calls for a love that is wiser and stronger and more lasting than any of these:

A love that is able to give sacrificially for the good of others.

A love that can see beyond the evil, the unworthy, the despicable.

A love that is strong and wise to do the best thing for the most at any time, including the worst.

A love able to meet opposition and persecution—to find joy even in facing a cross.

Such love is what Paul means in his Hymn to Love when he speaks of "charity," using the Greek word "agape." It is what the writer of I John meant when he said, "Let us love one another; for love is of God" (I John 4:7).

The great good news is that there is such love: It is pictured in the Suffering Servant passages in Isa. 53. It was revealed supremely in the Christ on his cross. It was reflected in those who like Paul believed that Christ in them was their hope of glory, who said of his fellow Jews, "I could wish myself accursed for the sake of my brethren." It was seen in Father Damien caring for the lepers until he himself became a leper, and in Albert Schweitzer leaving home and top recognition as a musician and theologian to minister to the native African. Is this weakness? Can we call this vice? No. This is truly the one hope of glory and life now and to come.

FREEDOM TO CARE

Where do we get this freedom to care responsibly? Certainly not from our own self-centered, unaided efforts. No man can pull himself up by his bootstraps, say, "Go to now and love like Christ" and succeed in this kind of loving.

Always through history, says Albert Camus, when man becomes his own god, he enslaves others. He cites many illustrations including the Jacobins during the French Revolution led by such sincere men as Saint Just. These men sought an abstract justice without God, which they set up as an absolute, and to this absolute principle they were willing to sacrifice everything. And in the name of justice they guillotined 250,000 Frenchmen!

In our own time how many brave young humanists set out to make a new world, but when disappointment, rejection, and persecution arise they can't take it. The need for this "strange form of love" is recognized by Plato, Socrates, and all other ancient and modern thinkers. The Roman, Seneca, taught it, but knuckled under to Nero and died a suicide in disgust at his own inability to live by his professed ideals. Another Roman, Ovid, testified in effect, "I know the better course; the worse is the one I follow." And Paul cried out in a frustration that is common to mankind, "I can will what is right, but I cannot do it. For I do not do the good I want, but the evil I do not want is what I do. . . . Wretched man that I am! Who will deliver me from this body of death?" (Rom. 7:18-19, 24). Then he witnesses to the victory over his frustration—the difference between Paul and Seneca— "Thanks be to God through Jesus Christ our Lord!" (Rom. 7:25). Thus he writes to the Ephesians of his great prayer which contains the finest insight yet known to man concerning the power to love:

For this reason I bow my knees before the Father . . . that according to the riches of his glory he may grant you to be strengthened with might through his Spirit in the inner man, and that Christ

67

may dwell in your hearts through faith; that you, being rooted and grounded in love, may have power to comprehend with all the saints what is the breadth and length and height and depth, and to know the love of Christ which passes knowledge [that is, beyond human knowledge unaided by the Spirit] (Eph. 3:14-19).

Human freedom to care responsibly at its best is a faith response to God's love in Christ; not only in Jesus two thousand years ago, but in those who truly follow him. Christ in us today—this was what gave Paul his power to love. He had never known Jesus in the flesh; but even as he watched Stephen die from the stones for which he was responsible, and saw him revealing the same love that made Jesus say "forgive them," Paul was moved to respond and himself to be overcome by Christ's love.

In differing ways but in the same spirit, men and women through all the ages have been set free to love. One of the most inspiring illustrations of this fact is the story of Ernest Gordon in his autobiographical account, *Through the Valley of the Kwai*. It is a deeply moving story of his experiences as captain of a company of Scotch Highlanders during their imprisonment by the Japanese in Thailand during World War II. During the first few weeks in which nearly half died of starvation,

Existence had become so miserable, the odds so heavy against us, that nothing mattered except to survive. We lived by the rule of the jungle, "red in tooth and claw"—the evolutionary law of the survival of the fittest. It was a case of "I look out for myself and to hell with everyone else.". . . The weak were trampled underfoot, the sick ignored or resented, the dead forgotten.

When a man lay dying we had no word of mercy. When he cried for our help, we averted our heads. Men cursed the Japanese, their neighbors, themselves, and God. Cursing became such an obsession that they contructed whole sentences in which every word was a curse.

Everyone was his own keeper. It was free enterprise at its worst, with all the restraints of morality gone.[10]

Then came a miracle. Two men gave their lives for their buddies. One, in a sudden heroic act, took the blame for a lost shovel that otherwise would have cost the lives of dozens of prisoners before machine guns. The Japanese captain shot him, but the others were saved. The other gave his life in a steady, loving, compassionate concern for his sick friends. He slipped out of camp and bartered with natives for food, giving it to his buddy who was sick until he himself died of starvation.

These two stories went around the camp and a new spirit took hold of the men. They began to share and to care. Ernest Gordon, himself ill with ulcers and edema from beriberi and sick with dysentery and diphtheria, asked to be moved to the "death house" because it was quieter and cleaner than the hospital. He was ministered to by a young boy, "Dusty," whom he had not known before. Friends moved him to a little hut which they had built outside the death house and Dusty washed his gangrenous sores and brought him food, thus saving his life.

One of the best evidences of a new life among the men was the formation of an orchestra. The Red Cross sent them a half-dozen violins—about the only things their captors allowed to get through. A few of the men had hidden a trumpet or a trombone through all the struggles, and now they brought them out. But most of them made their own instruments—a bass viol from tea box wood, the strings made from the intestines of cows from a slaughterhouse; kettledrums made out of oil drums hammered down to differing depths, with hides from the slaughterhouse stretched over them. They had no music, or paper to write it on, but some who had been musicians before they entered the war remembered enough of the music they had once played to write it down on the white insides of large bamboo sections.

The first concert was held at twilight on the side of the hill. It was a never-to-be-forgotten hour, with the emaciated faces of men once half dead now alive with joy as the beauty of Beethoven's *Fifth Symphony* and Gilbert and Sullivan's *The Mikado* lifted their hearts. After it was over there was silence, then tumultuous applause.

I glanced at my neighbor. His face was shining.
"Great! Isn't it great?" he exclaimed. . . . While they listened, faces came to life. . . . I heard a little skeleton of a man near me say to his companion with feeling, "God, that was lovely—bloody lovely!" I thought to myself as I heard it, "Aren't there two kinds of food—one for the body and one for the soul?". . . The music reminded us that there is always beauty to be found in life—even amid the ashes.[11]

Beauty out of ashes! The power to love in an evil time! An accident? Chance? To say so is to possess more credulity than I am able to accept. It was no accident nor chance. The power to love that came to these men under these trying circumstances was caught from the two men who died for them. Where did they get it? From others—perhaps their parents or others who influenced them in their youth, who in turn received it from others, and these others from Christ. Not just from the Christ who lived two thousand years ago, but from the living God who inspires all love and courage in every age.

Can't a man love his fellows without loving God? Up to a point, yes. But it seems from the experiences of all human history that such love in the crucial places is not at its best apart from the love of God.

But what about men such as Clarence Darrow and Albert Camus who say they don't believe in God or love him, but who do love their fellow man? The truth of the matter is that they are living by a faith which their intellect denies, which within itself is one of the strangest absurdities of human life. The truth is they do love the great Eternal Love that is at the heart of all things; but they do not call it God, and they would avoid the use of the word "Christ."

Here is one of the supreme facts of human experience: To be free to love even on a cross—free to share the source and inspiration of this love with others—comes most fully to one who loves because he has first been loved. And it is the love of God revealed in Christ that is most likely to develop this response. Martin Luther pointed out that we give God's love to others. When we do this we are like a pipe open at both ends. The love of God enters at the top and flows out at the bottom through our love to others.

In *The Nun's Story*, Illunga, a crazed young African boy, entered a Roman Catholic hospital in the Congo and killed a nun because a witch doctor told him he would not be freed from his dead wife's spirit unless he took a white woman's life. Emil, a native converted to Christianity, faced Sister Luke with shame and fear after the incident, amazed that she treated him no differently than before. "I don't understand. . . . If such a death happened to one of ours, Mama Luke, we would stake the murderer out along the riverbank and each fisherman would cut a piece of his flesh for bait until there was nothing left but his bones."

Sister Luke replied, "You *would* have, Emil, if . . . you were not wearing that sign of Him who taught us to forgive." [12]

In the movie, Sister Luke's real test came in Belgium during the war after her father, a kindly doctor, was killed by the Nazis as he ministered to the wounded. Now she found herself bitter and unable to forgive. One day she went into the church and as she waited she saw beyond the One hanging on the cross to the love of God. Then she was able to forgive and to minister in love to the wounded Nazis.

The only hope for the bitterness of Africa, Cleveland, Birmingham, and Columbus is the "love, which binds everything together in perfect harmony." I do not say that such love has been found nowhere except among Christians, but I do believe that it has been revealed in its most effective and highest form with the inspiration of the One whom we call the Christ.

Jerome, one of the early church fathers, interpreting Paul's prayer through which man comes to know the breadth and length, height and depth of the love of Christ, describes the Cross as a symbol of this mighty love of God: One arm represents the *breadth* of God's love: including all mankind, all races, colors, groups, nations. The other arm represents the *length* to which this love will go, even to the valley of suffering, shame, and death. The top of the cross represents the *height* of the love of God, including all the universe. In whatever is beyond the sun and stars there is love like that of Christ. The bottom part of the cross represents the depth of God's love which reaches down to the lowest depths of human failure and need. There is no situation even in the hell of fear and hate that is untouched by the depth of the love of Christ. This is the basic structure of reality which is our hope.

I am set free to love when I respond by an act of faith to the great love of God that is from everlasting to everlasting, and that never fails. As part of my response I will choose my vocation, I will build my home, I will make small as well as great choices in a way which will best express this love.

> O love that will not let me go,
> I rest my weary soul in Thee;
> I give Thee back the life I owe,
> That in Thine ocean depths its flow
> May richer, fuller be.[13]

> Were the whole realm of nature mine,
> That were an offering far too small;
> Love so amazing, so divine,
> Demands my soul, my life, my all.[14]

the ABSURDITY
of UNBELIEF

You and I live and breathe, suffer and die on the edge of vast absurdities. Sometimes we are more conscious of them than at other times. Sometimes they would really be laughable, if they were not at the same time so tragic. Is there a way to transcend the absurdities, see them for what they are and laugh at them? This would be a priceless power indeed, for then we might meet them wisely and courageously.

One of my favorite stories is that of the old man in a small village who had suffered greatly in the loss of family and property. Like all other human beings the loss had cost him dearly. But after a time of struggle and agony, he began to live as the most cheerful and adequate person in the entire community. Marveling at his recovery, his friends asked him how it was he could be so calm and joyful when everything had gone wrong. The old man replied, "Well, whenever I begin to feel sorry for myself and start to worry, I just crawl up on a fence and watch myself pass by and I just die laughing!"

At what was he laughing? Not at his pain and suffering— that is not a laughing matter for anyone—but at his foolish, absurd lapse into self-pity and doubt, fear and resentment by which he denied the wealth of his resources and the joy and love that were still his. For he was first and primarily a man of faith, committed to and trusting in the God of Christ, in whom he found meaning and hope and the power to love. It was his ability to pray and worship, to think in the perspective of such living faith that gave him a fence upon which to climb so that he could laugh at himself.

How greatly you and I need such a fence from which to view our human farce. For we too suffer anguish and loss, pain and trouble, frustration and defeat. The question is, can we learn from it? As we look at our foolish attitudes and acts, we may do either one of two things: We may either laugh or cry. Either we find a fence upon which we may climb to see above the absurdities to the meaning and values that are real, so that we laugh at the absurdities and rise over them to a living faith and a significant life and a victorious death, or else we fight the absurdities and give up in hopelessness and despair as finally we are overwhelmed and conquered by them. We may take our choice.

People in all ages always have lived on the edge of the absurd, whether or not they have been aware of it; but since the beginning of the Atomic Age with all of the scientific possibilities of this wonderful universe, the razor's edge of human absurdity is sharper today that in any other time in history. Man has always had mighty expectations in comparison with his pitiably small achievements. This has been true whether we are freshmen in college or octogenarians nearing the sundown of life. This is at the same time our glory and our misery, the reason we have done such amazingly difficult and creative things and the reason for our greatest suffering.

AN HONEST FAITH FOR OUR TIME

With all our many human absurdities, what and where is the fence upon which we can climb to view our human situation so that we may get a perspective with meaning that adds significance to our human struggle? That is the question of all questions—the question we are really asking of those who would teach us. This is the goal of all true education: not only competence and knowledge but meaning, to enable us to choose the highest, truest values and live by them.

Christians through the centuries have claimed that faith in the God of our Lord Jesus Christ is this fence from which believers may find meaning out of meaninglessness, love out of lovelessness, hope out of despair, and peace out of confusion.

In our scientific age, however, there are literally millions of people who consider themselves intelligent, thinking persons, who declare that such a belief in a Christlike God is the height of all human absurdities. Back in Old Testament times and even no farther back than the days of our forefathers, belief in God was rarely questioned. The writers in the Old and New Testaments never thought it was necessary to prove the existence of God. "The fool hath said in his heart, There is no God," says the fourteenth Psalm. He was assured that God is the Creator and Sustainer of the world.

"But after all," modern man cries, "the people back in those

76

ancient times did not know as much about the universe as we do. Theirs was a tidy little world with the heavens above and hell beneath. God was off in the heavens sitting on a throne. But here in this scientific age, it sounds foolish to talk about any God of purpose and love." Oh, we may accept God as an Integrating Principle, or Cosmic Force, or as some built-in System of Natural Law that accidentally got going billions of years ago and in due time will be extinguished. But to many of us, all the faith by which millions have lived and died—faith in a loving, Christlike God who is better than the best human father—is considered absurd! In olden days a man was considered a fool not to believe in God. Often today a man who believes is called a fool!

This does not mean that such moderns would not like very much to believe if they could. Indeed, they would be very happy to have the comfort of believing in a wise, loving, heavenly Father; but the whole environment in which they live makes it seem difficult, if not impossible. They cannot see how they can live in such a scientific world and honestly and intelligently accept such a belief. So for many (including some who go to church), to all intents and purposes of actual living, God is dead. They may mourn his passing and feel sad about it, but to believe otherwise indeed seems folly!

Is there then such a valid faith? we ask. How can we find an honest, meaningful faith for our times? Can we as intelligent, thinking persons in a scientific age find a fence of faith upon which we may take our stand that will give perspective and meaning to our lives? Indeed, we may! This is my sure and wholehearted conviction. In fact, with all my heart I believe that unbelief in a God who is like Christ is of

77

all human absurdities the most absurd! The verdict of human history and experience as I see it declares that such unbelief is the supreme human folly!

This is not to say that all doubt and unbelief are bad. Indeed, a healthy doubt, an honest disbelief of the things that need doubting, are the first requirements for a healthy faith. We need to ask questions, honestly and frankly, about things that ought to be questioned. We need to doubt, and then we need to question our doubting. We need to have the same approach to life as we have when we go into a laboratory: an open-mindedness toward the truth. The only way we can understand or know whether or not a thing is true is as we test it in our experience. I am not pleading for the preservation of superstition, but for the open-mindedness toward and the willingness to act on the deepest and highest truths revealed in human experience—truths which can be known and acted upon just as surely as in the physical and material realms. We know this faith is the best approach to reality because when we act upon it we find ourselves and our neighbors. Then life at its highest increasingly is ours.

UNBELIEF AND THE ABSURD

There are three kinds of unbelief, which I believe are absurd:

First, there is *the absurdity of the unbelief which we may call Moral Doubt*. There are many who assent intellectually to what they call faith in God as revealed in Christ; but their daily lives are in moral and spiritual rebellion against what their lips profess. According to John Baillie, many are believers with the tops of their minds, but atheists from the bottom of their minds! [1]

78

This was the kind of unbelief of which the writer of Ps. 14 was speaking when he said, "The fool hath said . . . , There is no God." Since no one at the time really questioned the existence of God or gods, he probably meant, "There is no God here and now who is going to judge or influence me." This is what Jeremiah was saying of many of the inhabitants of Jerusalem:

> They have spoken falsely of the Lord
> and have said, "He will do nothing" (Jer. 5:12).

So also doubters have said all through the centuries. The writer of Psalm 42 speaks of those who cry contemptuously, "Where is your God?"

We all have asked the same question at times. Without doubting for a moment that God exists, we still ask, "Where is he? Why doesn't he do something about all the evils and injustices?" We truly would like to believe in God as just and loving and as good as Christ, but there is one major block that prevents it. If we did believe with our whole hearts, we would have to answer the moral summons to obey the truth and to love even as we are loved, and this we definitely are not ready to do. So, instead of honestly admitting that we do not want to believe because it is too costly, we rationalize our unwillingness to act by faith and deceive ourselves into thinking that we really doubt the existence of God!

Harry Emerson Fosdick describes a letter from a young woman who said in effect, "You are always talking about the peace of mind which faith in God brings, but I want you to know that since I have given up my belief in God I have never had such peace of mind!"

Well, of course her belief in God was troublesome. It always is, until and unless we commit ourselves to live by our faith. What she meant was that at last she had rationalized her unwillingness to live by the strong demands her faith in God made upon her. Now that she had at last intellectually renounced God, she was not bothered by her conscience.

> She set a rose to blossom in her hair,
>   The day Faith died—
> "Now glad," she said, "and free at last, I go,
>   And life is wide."
> But through long nights she stared into the dark
>   And knew she lied.[2]

I believe we cannot live any kind of meaningful, worthy life except as we live not just with the top of our minds but with the bottom of our minds and hearts set on our faith in God— the source of the highest God we know!

Here is the main reason many of us do not find God real, even though we think we believe in him: because we are unwilling to do his will.

Another and opposite kind of unbelief that is equally absurd is from the top of the mind: intellectual unbelief. There are many very sincere people who simply cannot believe intellectually in the God of Christ.

Atheism had its beginnings back in the days of the Sophists of Athens in the fourth century B.C. Plato, who once declared that all known races believed in God, described the unbelief of these Sophists as something new in the thinking of man.

In one of his stories he tells of an Athenian tourist (obviously Plato himself) on the island of Crete, talking with

Celinias, a native of the island. He is telling the Cretan about the atheists. Celinias suggests that all doubt of God is due to "lack of self-control in the matter of pleasures and desires." But the Athenian answers that there must be another cause, "a certain very grievous sort of ignorance, which nevertheless wears the appearance of being wisdom."

There is plenty of this kind of atheistic doubt today from very sincere minds, from people who think they are exceedingly wise but are afflicted with "a very grievous sort of ignorance." Paul described such ignorance: "Knowing God, they have refused to honour him as God, or to render him thanks. Hence all their thinking has ended in futility [absurdity], and their misguided minds are plunged in darkness. They boast of their wisdom, but they have made fools of themselves!" (Rom. 1:21-22, NEB.)

Today there are not only those who disbelieve in God because they are unwilling to face the moral challenges their faith demands, but also there are those who live and act as though the God of love and truth is the nature of reality. Since they live in a day of scientific testing when everything must be proved, they cannot accept intellectually the God of strong, wise love. They live by more faith than their lips profess. They believe more in God from the bottom of their mind than from the intellectual top of it.

This is obviously one of the most absurd positions anyone can hold, as a man by the name of Job found out back in the Old Testament drama. He felt God was unjust. Though he had lived a good life, he had great suffering, having lost his family, his property, and now suffered the pains of boils over his body! Troubled by the conflict between justice and love of God, he rebelled at God and cried out in effect, as doubters do today, "I will keep my own integrity, though I can't stand the injustice of God (his lack of integrity). I will work for justice even though there is no God of Justice."

We must admit there is something attractive, even noble about such persons. We cannot but admire the ancient Job, or the modern Clarence Darrow who spent his life defending the underdog, practicing the love of truth and justice, but to his dying day refused to believe with the top of his mind that there was any God as good as himself! While on the one hand this is noble, it is on the other hand absurd, as Job began to realize: the very idea of a little man claiming to be better and more just than his Creator, better than anything in all creation!

"Who is this that darkens counsel by words without knowledge?" a voice asked Job.

> Gird up your loins like a man,
>   I will question you. . . .
> Where were you when I laid the foundation of the earth? . . .
> Have you commanded the morning . . .
>   and caused the dawn to know its place? . . .
> Can you bind the chains of the Pleiades,
>   or loose the cords of Orion?

In the great and humbling experience that followed, Job cried at last,

> I have uttered what I did not understand,
>   things too wonderful for me, which I did not know
>   (see Job 38-42).

It is truly absurd to believe that mine is the finest, best, and highest wisdom in all creation! How proudly, like a peacock, man struts around until some of his tail feathers are plucked! And yet some fine humanitarians and fighters for justice have been afflicted with "this grievous ignorance" that kept them from accepting with the top of their minds what the bottom of their minds already believed and acted upon! Yes, a few people have a great deal more faith than they profess; and some profess a lot more than they live. Both kinds of unbelief are absurd.

There is a third kind of unbelief which is both from the top and bottom of our minds and hearts—intellectual and moral atheism—which is tragic indeed. And pathetically absurd.

Many persons have begun with intellectual atheism. Rebelling, as did Job, at the contradictions of life, they have cried out in utter defiance: "If there is a God, I can't stand the injustices he permits or perpetrates." They may, and often do, go on further to say: "Therefore there is no God, I believe in nothing but the accidental collocation of atoms—the formation of the universe and man by the laws of chance. Therefore nothing has any meaning except as I and other men put it there. There is no transcendent reason for living. I keep on living, without knowing why, or even asking; for there is no why or whence or wherefore. Therefore I hate life, or God, or whatever has made this meaningless universe and my inadequacy." There is a great deal of this hatred of life even among youth of today, not to speak of those who have grown old fighting it. They are depressed, bored, fed up—sick of life!

Their rebellion may give a certain freedom and peace for the moment. How many a person without such a faith has had to admit with young Philip in W. Somerset Maugham's auto-biographical novel, *Of Human Bondage*, that "the power that possessed him seemed to have nothing to do with reason," or with the sense of "I ought" which suggests that one can choose one's course by an effort of will. And that reason is the surest guide. Philip admitted that he did not follow his reason nor obey his conscience. He was a slave of his passions, "a slave because I can't help myself." [3] What a familiar ring this has for some of us!

Paul had the power to conquer his passions and to live the life of love and Philip did not, because of what Carl Jung, father of modern analytical psychiatry, called the presence of faith, hope, and love in something ultimate beyond himself. Where Paul had "Christ through faith dwelling in his heart in love," Philip had nothing but meaninglessness. Born with a clubfoot, fighting the cruelty and injustice of life and others, he was indeed in bondage to his passions. The only small happiness that came to him was when at last he decided to accept the fact that for him there was "no meaning in life, and man by living served no end. . . . Life was insignificant and death without consequence."

This gave him for a time an exulting sense of being free: "It seemed to him that the last burden of responsibility was taken from him. . . . His insignificance was turned to power, and he felt himself suddenly equal with the cruel fate which had seemed to persecute him."

But it was a freedom of irresponsibility, and it was power not to help and heal, but to hurt; and he did hurt himself and other people.

What he did or left undone did not matter. Failure was unimportant and success amounted to nothing. He was the most inconsiderate creature in that swarming mass of mankind which for a brief space occupied the surface of the earth; and he was almighty because he had wrenched from chaos the secret of its nothingness. . . . "O life," he cried in his heart, "O life, where is thy sting?" [4]

But this happiness and freedom was brief and short-lived—for his irresponsibility led him to do many things that hurt and stung others and himself. Only when at last through what could only be called the Christlike love of a young woman he began to think of "the man dying on the Cross who cried, 'Father forgive them, they know not what they do'"—only then did he begin to find meaning, and with it the power to love.

In the end, with other rebels against God and life, we hate ourselves and everything about us for this meaningless, inadequate life. There are many variations of this rebellion from the beatniks in Greenwich Village to the intellectual giants such as Nietzsche, Sartre, and Heidegger. One of the best descriptions of the absurdity of such unbelief is that given by Ivan in Dostoevski's *The Brothers Karamazov*. He had suffered great injustices, including some evil things done to him by his father. After losing faith in God, finally Ivan came to the point where he decided that it was all right for him to kill his father. Said Ivan, "I only know that suffering exists, that no one is guilty, that everything is connected, that everything passes away and equals out." [5]

Since everything equals out, therefore everything is permitted! Hence I will do what I want to do. If I want to accept what society calls virtue and morality, all right; but if I want to rebel and kill and destroy, what does it matter? Such a position cuts the roots of any worthy and responsible action of living whatever!

WHEN DOUBT IS DIFFICULT

Beyond the moral consequences of the loss of a meaningful faith, there are two other reasons why these three kinds of unbelief are absurd:

First, because *such deadening unbelief is unnecessary*, contrary to the idea held by many sincere persons who feel that atheism, or at best, agnosticism, is necessary if they are to continue to live honestly and intelligently in the present-day scientific world. But how absurd and unscientific can you get?

It is indeed irrational and inconsistent in the name of science to "limit trustworthy knowledge to judgments which are reached through the methods of the exact sciences." [6] And yet this is what these unbelievers feel compelled to do in the name of science.

Of course, in the exact sciences, only the judgments that can be measured by the microscope, the telescope, the test tube or in some other tangible way are accepted—so-called "objective judgments." All value judgments supposedly are excluded. But in the realm of personality where we live and move and have our being, we refuse every day to use only the methods of exact science.

Imagine two young people in love, scientifically trying to measure or prove their love for each other by examining the chemical reaction of their blood, or the nervous energy released by the brain as shown by an electroencephalograph.

They had better examine their own heads! For if they use that approach, they will surely lose love. Most things of value in life cannot be measured by exact sciences. No, for in the realm of personal and social living, "judgments of value, far from being disturbing factors, become the instruments, through which alone trustworthy knowledge can be had." [7]

Science has not excluded religion or made impossible a faith in a God who is like Christ! To the contrary, science has made faith in God even more important, more necessary. For what is faith in God but that set of ultimate values to which we give our highest allegiance? Without some such living faith most thinking persons know there would not be any world to inhabit. It is the height of absurdity to think of leaving mankind and his world to the fate of Frankenstein monsters created by those who know only the exact sciences. If science is defined as the method of honestly seeking and openheartedly obeying the truth, then the Christian faith is the highest and most important science of all. We do not find that highest truth by which life is meaningful and worth living by using a test tube or a telescope, but by using the methods of mental, moral, and spiritual experience through which the deepest realities may become known and obeyed. The truth has been tested by the experience of mankind throughout the centuries.

Second, unbelief in either of these three ways is absurd, not only because it is unnecessary, but because it leads to deification of men. Such deification of man has never yet failed to produce demons instead of angels, for it leads to the loss of both freedom and justice. Even Albert Camus, whom many regard as an atheist, came to this conclusion. When man ceases to believe in God, he makes himself into a sort of God. And when man becomes God, others more often than not become his slaves. Through history this has been the result of rebellious unbelief.[8] The real test of faith in God or faith in man without God is what happens to the values by which life is significant and meaningful under both. The denial of God destroys these values—so the history of the past one hundred years declares with terrifying clarity.

There are two extremes to which faith in man without God takes us, both of which are absurd:

The first is what might be called *extreme relativism*,[9] where everything of value is relative to everything else, the products of historical development, or cultural or national influences, and therefore cease to have any real claim on my commitment and allegiance. I might just as well say with James Stephens,

> Good and bad and right and wrong
> Wave the silly words away:
> This is wisdom to be strong,
> This is virtue to be gay.[10]

Granted, many of the moral codes as specific experiences of value are relative up to a point; but a basic stance of all religious faith is that there are ultimate values such as reverence for life and respect for persons rooted in the nature of all existence. What kind of enduring and worthwhile life can be built on the stance of extreme relativism? If nothing is ultimate then nothing commands me and I am lost in boredom and meaninglessness. No home or nation can long endure the murky maze of such relativism.

Or my unbelief may take me to what may be called *posi-*

tivism. Since human life needs something absolute and ultimate by which to live and die, and since there is no God to
represent the ultimate, then I must choose some objective
reality or value which I make supreme—such as the state or
the party or the leader or some abstract value such as justice
or freedom. These I make my gods. But where God is not, man
is not.

Suppose, for instance, we make justice our God and determine to take it in our own hands as did the French revolu-
tionists and as the Marxists have done in Russia, China, and
Cuba? We end up by destroying freedom and we produce
more injustice than we had in the beginning. Or suppose we
make freedom our God and go out to be free of all restrictions?
The result is anarchy and the loss of all freedom.

Without God we sink into nihilism, where there is a nothingness for which to live or die. And then it does not matter
what we do, good or bad, noble or ignoble. It all depends on
what we want at the moment. Life is stripped of meaning
when God is dead. As Emil Brunner puts it, "Man has spirit
only in that he is addressed by God. . . . Therefore the human
self is nothing which exists in its own right." [11] Only when we
are in loving, trusting relationship to God are we alive and
whole!

WHERE GOD BECOMES NECESSSARY

Any way we look at it, nothing is more irrational and absurd
than the refusal or neglect to live and act by conscious faith in
a God of Christlike love. Why? Let me state it positively:
Because only such faith makes possible the acceptance and

sustaining of meaning and value without which human life at its best is impossible or at least not worth living.

We have used several illustrations of this fact of human experience in the preceding pages. Here are two more:

First, in the handling of our failures and/or sins, what do we do with persons who have broken the moral as well as the social laws of the community, and have not only sinned against custom but against themselves and others? Here is the woman taken in the act of adultery brought before Jesus by the Pharisees. "The law of Moses says, 'Stone her.' What do you say?" Now an extreme relativist would have said, "It doesn't matter. Adultery is just the breaking of a temporary moral code. Forget it!" On the other hand, a positivist might have joined with the Scribes and Pharisees in saying, "The important thing is preserving the custom of family loyalty. Give her justice. The law says 'Stone her,' so let's get on with the stoning." But Jesus had compassion on her and said, "Let him that is without sin cast the first stone. . . . Go and sin no more." Jesus' faith in God as righteous Father brought the true value that went beyond both relativism and positivism. In effect, he was saying, "It is wrong to be indifferent to the violation of human personality which adultery represents; but it is just as wrong to be merciless in the demand for rigid justice. Forgiving love is better than either, for it contains both justice and freedom. Forgive her as God forgives and help her to a new life which respects persons and is respected." This is the highest good.

Such mediation and reconciliation between contradiction— what the Greeks called "moderation"—is the priceless requirement for any healthy personal or social life. Finding the third viewpoint (the highest good, God's viewpoint) is possible only to one who has faith that there is such a viewpoint grounded in the very nature of life. Only an intelligent faith in the God who gives and expects of us a strong wise love can provide the wisdom and the courage to live the good life.

The second illustration of this truth is seen in the question being asked not only by sociologists and penologists, but by parents: How do we go beyond punishment for the breaking of moral and social laws? How do we right wrongs in the wrongdoer and bring growth out of selfishness and imperfection?

As a boy of five, I was dressed one Sunday morning in my best white sailor suit and told by my mother to be careful for a few minutes while she completed her preparations for going to church. But there was a delightful mud puddle in the back yard. I tried to jump over it, but fell in the middle of it, much to my mother's horror.

Suppose she had given me strict justice and in anger had spanked me, demanding that I never, never do that again? Very likely the spanking would have done me little or no good, nor would it have helped my mother; for the very next time I would likely have gone out to do it again just to prove that I could!

Or suppose she had given me a completely permissive freedom out of a soft love. She could have wiped away my tears as she dressed me in a clean suit. "Oh, don't worry! Everything is all right." That would not have been love, but rather the most unkind thing she could have done; for it would have helped me to grow into a self-centered little tyrant, expecting to be petted and allowed to have my own way, only to break my heart against a world not run for my convenience.

But what my mother gave me was loving justice. "Yes, it was a bad thing you did. Because I love you I will have to punish you, in order to help you remember that we are all in the family together and must help each other instead of making more work for the other." She took off my dirty clothes and administered the punishment, but as she did, I knew my wrong hurt her because she loved me. Without any formulation in words I knew that not my punishment alone, but her own suffering love had helped to right the wrong I had done. I was filled with a strange peace, a delicious sense of belonging to a family where each one was important, each one cared for the other. And I decided that I would not hurt my mother like that again. I was determined to be a better person.

In this simple childhood experience, multiplied a hundred times, is God's way of righting wrongs, whether in the home, or among friends, in the community, or the society, the nation or the world. Without loving justice there are always two evils: first, the wrong action and then, the wrong reaction. Compounded, they make the evil not twice as destructive, but sometimes ten or a hundred times. The application of loving justice is never easy and requires a perspective that transcends both our positions.

Indeed, the success of our American government and way of life, or any other system of human cooperation, depends entirely on the reconciliation of contradictions. We need both justice and freedom. Man is meant to be free, but such freedom without responsibility is anarchy without justice. So we have the Declaration of Independence and the Constitution and its amendments, which declare that all men are created free and equal before God. We established the representative legislature to make the laws, the executive branch to administer them, and the Supreme Court to interpret and adjudicate between them.

That is, we succeed as a democracy only through checks and balances by which we keep the razor's edge of freedom with justice. In the last analysis, this is possible only through the possession by enough of the people of this strange form of love without which any rebellion leads to anarchy and destruction.

Where do we get reconciliation of contradictions—the ability to find meaning and moderation between the conflicts and absurdities of human life? Only from the God who put into our very nature the need for "the Love that will not let us go." It is absurd that Albert Camus, Clarence Darrow, and others, with their lives and acts had a faith in the God of love which their lips and words denied!

Yes, we must have moderation between the extremes. We need morals and principles, but also we need a strange love to reconcile the contradictions and to keep us steady even in the midst of injustices and imperfections in our lives and homes, our nation and world. We need to be rebels at injustice and evil, but we need to do so without making a farce of life.

The most important single aim in life should be to dig beneath the secondhand faith that believes only from the top of the mind or the absurd unbelief we have inherited from a pseudo-scientific environment to a first-hand faith that accepts the meaning, courage, and hope that has made life beautiful to countless thousands in every age.

FINDING the
GOALPOSTS

In life, as in aviation and in sports, there are many stories of "Wrong-Way Corrigans," who, like the fabled aviator, took off in the wrong direction! Or like the football hero who ran the wrong way because he didn't know where the goalposts were! Unlike him they are not addled by a blow on the head, but by a blow in the mind. The loss of moral and spiritual goalposts in our world today is another tragic absurdity resulting from man's loss of a living faith in God.

For faith in God is the willingness to act on the conviction that there are goalposts in the game of life; that is, that there is a moral order in our human existence that, when accepted and obeyed, gives meaning and direction to our living.

But we are living in a day of little or no vital faith in God on the part of millions. Hence there are many who have little or no morals except the mores or customs of the group to which they belong. We are rebels today, but of a different sort than those of the 1920's. The post-World-War-I rebels were violently opposed to a Victorian morality which was very concrete and clearly defined, whereas the rebels of the 1960's have only the barest remnants of a code that is not even well-defined by the preachers and educators, much less by parents. The United States, says one educator, is engaged in "an orgy of open-mindedness."

True, there still are parents and churches that proclaim occasionally the relevance of the Ten Commandments and what they call "the Christian attitude toward sex" and other moral questions; but too often even they are confused as to what they really mean. It is a rare parent indeed who has both the standards and a faith that gives meaning to moral convictions.

On the other hand there are many more who by seeking for "new standards for a new age," are indicating that the old standards are gone. As one current magazine reports, this is an era

in which morals are widely held to be both private and relative, in which pleasure is increasingly considered an almost constitutional right rather than a privilege, in which self-denial is increasingly seen as foolishness rather than virtue. . . . [The new gospel is the] message that sex will save you and libido make you free.[1]

Many moderns have little to rebel against except the meaninglessness of a game without any goalposts—and perhaps this is the most absurd and devastating of all kinds of rebellion. If life is without God, it is also without any meaning except what each one puts into it at the moment. If it is without meaning it is without morals. And without morals we are lost in the swamps of relativism where nothing makes sense or has any value. And this, of all things, our humanity is not able to stand.

"BECAUSE—THEREFORE"

We can stand almost anything if we believe there is meaning in it—that there is a real connection between the cause and the result. Life's meaning hangs on the way we use two simple conjunctions: "because . . . therefore." These words or their equivalent stand out in the writings of the prophet Jeremiah and all through the Bible. They are also words with which we in our scientifically minded age are certainly familiar.

If we know the cause we are able to deal with it. Conversely, we can't stand life's blows or even life's monotony when we feel there isn't any meaning to it all. When life is nonsensical, it is hard to take.

This is the reason science is so welcome to the minds of men. For if we know the cause of some evil effect, we have hopes of doing something to remove it. For this reason millions of dollars are being spent on cancer research to find the "million-murdering cause." Once it is isolated, we may find a cure for cancer. "Because of this . . . and this . . . a definite result may be expected." This is great ground for hope.

We are at home in a world of scientific cause and effect. We may rest confidently on certain dependable assumptions about our physical universe. The sad and tragic fact is that millions of people today are cynical and disillusioned about the moral and spiritual world. They have lost the connection between any "because" and "therefore" in their living, a connection which our forefathers were so confident existed. Everything is relative. There seem to be no fixed stars to steer our course by. For so many people there is no moral and spiritual framework with the Living God underneath. They are not sure what is right and what is wrong. "If only we knew what was truly good for us and our families and our world!" they cry. If only our personal and social existence could be lived in such a tidy world of cause and effect as our physical and material lives are based!

We acknowledge the deep need for a framework of meaning with understandable causes and clearly defined effects.

How important this is in our family relationships is obvious. Children who grow up without limits, direction, or discipline, whose parents say, "Oh, do anything you want, just stay out of my hair," generally end up as delinquents, and finally as adult criminals. Our children want and need discipline, to know the limits, the right and wrong of things and why.

So do we all need a framework of meaning in life. How can you play a good game in life when you don't even know where the goalposts are? The good parent is the one who teaches the child to see the real goalposts when it comes to physical, mental, moral, and spiritual well-being. "Because you want healthy teeth, therefore you brush your teeth night and morning." And fortunately when it comes to teeth, we have some horrible examples. We may point to one and say, "Because he didn't brush his teeth, therefore he has decay and must make many trips to the dentist." Or we may say to our school children, "Because you want to be able to make a good living and a worthy contribution in life, you study hard."

It is even more desirable for the good parent to be able to say to the child, "Because we want to know our true selves and to discover the conditions of the good life; therefore we will keep our minds open to know as much of God as we can know in worship, prayer, and study."

Look what happens when without a vital faith in God we have no adequate goals for living. There is no meaningful purpose that connects our desires and actions with the appropriate results? Suppose we just drift along following the desires that promise the most pleasure and the avoidance of the most pain, saying, "Because I want this, therefore I will do this," but with no overall view of the limits and the goalposts. Obviously there is no likelihood of any creative or worthwhile life here. Certainly the bottom drops out when crises come and life is without ultimate meaning and value.

A young woman wrote to Sherwood Eddy,

A life without meaning, without aim, without eternity, with nothing but human pleasures, was disgusting to me. It was then that I saw the notice of your lectures on *The Meaning of Life, A Rational Basis for Religion*, etc. I went, and on returning, I went to sleep for the first time during the last two months without thought of suicide. Since then I have attended all your lectures. I now read the Bible daily and am again able to pray. I do not know what the future will be, but now I desire again to live. In any case, I shall prolong my life for the next three months to make the test of Jesus Christ by reading the Gospels once more and making the experiment you suggested. Pray for me.[2]

I do not know how the story ended, but from my own experience I am confident that if she made the test she found the meaning—and began to live.

I also know that all of us hunger for an adequate "because"

for our "therefores." J.B., the modern Job, keeps insisting in all his suffering that there must be meaning in it somewhere:

If I
Knew . . . If I knew why!
What I can't bear is this blindness—
Meaninglessnes—the numb blow
Fallen in the stumbling night! [3]

He does not know what the meaning is; but he holds on stubbornly to his faith in God, that such suffering must have a cause, a why. He never finds an adequate answer to the why, but he is sustained to the end by his faith in God so that he has a "therefore" to live by.

Viktor Frankl, the Austrian Jewish psychiatrist, describes this experience in a Nazi death camp. He says that the ones who gave up and died were the ones who could see no meaning at all in their situation. The ones who lived, like Job and J.B., found an ultimate meaning to cling to. Frankl has developed a new kind of psychotherapy called logotherapy, by which he seeks to cure the mentally sick by helping them find a meaning and purpose in life. His method comes from his own experience. When he was arrested, the Nazis destroyed his precious manuscript for a major book over which he had labored for years. He was thrown into the concentration camp in Bavaria to die like the rest:

Later, I remember, it seemed to me that I would die in the near future. In this critical situation . . . [the concern for most comrades] was "Will we survive the camp? For if not, all this suffering has no meaning." The question which beset me was, "Has all this suffering, this dying around us, a meaning? For, if not, then ultimately there is no meaning to survival; for a life whose meaning depends upon such a happenstance—whether one escapes or not —ultimately would not be worth living at all." [4]

Without some ultimate "because" there can be no worthy "therefore"!

THERE IS A MORAL ORDER

Faith in God as revealed in Christ is the willingness to act on the conviction that there are goalposts in the game of life; and as we have said, that God is more than impersonal goalposts. He is also the Impartial Referee and the Coach who knows both the rules and the players. To know something about the game, we need to know the Coach and be taught the rules and enter into the true spirit of the game.

Obviously, we are using another set of symbols to describe the basic meaning of human existence. The specifics in any analogy, of course, cannot be pressed too far or the analogy misrepresents and distorts. But the figure of life as a game with goalposts may be helpful in an area where there is untold confusion.

God as the Creator-Referee-Coach was described by Jeremiah, Isaiah, and Hosea and revealed by Jesus as One who loves the players with an everlasting love and gets into the game with us to help us make the goals and win. Here the analogy stops. For all games except the game of life require that there be losers. But life is a game in which everyone who will may win: "Whosoever will, let him take the water of life freely" (Rev. 22:17, KJV). That is, anyone who will love the Coach, be responsive to him, have an open mind, a willingness to be taught, a willingness to work and practice and do his

100

best to abide by the rules and when he fails, try again—anyone who will can make the goals and win in life!

Faith in the God of Christ is faith that there is meaning, "that nothing walks with aimless feet." Nothing is purely accidental. True, there are infinite chances taken in our personal lives as in the physical universe. The biggest chance of all was in the creation of man with freedom of thought, of will, and of choice. But all these chances are within the framework of a mighty purpose. There is a "because-therefore" in every area of life! This is the priceless stance of those who live by faith in God.

We can see this clearly in the so-called "order of nature." There is an order, though it is more flexible than we once thought. There is in it a field of indeterminacy and discontinuity as well as of continuity. Laws are only approximate, but they are still sure enough to be dependable. Once science thought of all things as an unbreakable chain of cause and effect. Darwin's *Origin of Species* seemed to leave out God altogether.

"As natural selection acts solely by accumulating slight, successive, favorable variations, it can produce no great or sudden modifications; it can act only by short and slow steps. Hence the canon of 'Natura non facit saltum' (Nature does not make a leap)." [5] Where do you need God in that, except maybe in the very beginning?

But today, most biologists and anthropologists believe that there are big leaps in the evolutionary order. Some of us believe that these, as well as the continuing growth, simply cannot be explained, except by the creative Mind we call God. We cannot accept the impossible view that it all is an accident.

What causes it? "In the beginning God," is the way the Bible describes the cause. "In the beginning God"—along the way God—God at each leap, mutation, variation; no matter how small and gradual or large and sudden, God guides the destiny of the universe and man. What a priceless "because-therefore" to give meaning in all our experiences. It is far more rational than any idea that chance or accident could have produced such results.

Because God wills it, the universe as we know it is here. Because God willed it, the brain capacity of man jumped from 300 cc. to 1500 cc. in a relatively short time. Because God willed it, there is a blessed correspondence in our spirits with his spirit.

Therefore, we who are creatures of this creative God have goalposts—principles or laws which summarize the conditions by which we can fulfill our purposes or refuse to do so. There is a cause for rain, snow, tides, winter, spring, as well as earthquakes and other natural evils; therefore we may adjust to these events. In the same way there is a "because-therefore" in our human events. Our human evils are not accidents. One man put it thus: "When a machine creaks, shudders, shakes, fails to perform efficiently, it is a victim either of bad design or bad management. But when a man is gloomy, grouchy, bad-tempered and depressed, he is most likely a victim of his own bad thinking." [6] (Or perhaps of withdrawal symptoms from quitting smoking cigarettes or of eating too much!)

So, when families crack and break, nations decay, society degenerates, a world explodes in a big war or boils over in a rash of little ones, it is because of our human ignorance or our willful disobedience.

The people of Judah asked Jeremiah, "Why is the land ruined and laid waste like a wilderness, so that no one passes through?" And Jeremiah interpreted the Lord's answer:

Because they have forsaken my law which I set before them, and have not obeyed my voice, or walked in accord with it, but have stubbornly followed their own hearts and have gone after the Baals.... *Therefore* thus says the Lord ... Behold, I will feed this people with wormwood, and give them poisonous water to drink. ... And now, *because* you have done all these things, says the Lord, and when I spoke to you persistently you did not listen ... therefore I will do to the house which is called by my name.... I will cast you out of my sight (Jer. 9:13-15; 7:13-14, italics added).

So back in the time of the depression, we too might have asked, "Why is the land ruined and laid waste?" And God was saying, "*Because* the people have disobeyed my voice, would not listen, and have gone after the Baals of money and pleasure with little concern for their neighbor; *therefore* is this come upon you."

God forbid that America should ever fall; but if we do, it will be because we have forsaken God's laws and refused to listen to his voice in the moral and spiritual order. If we come through these difficult times, it will be because we have listened, learned, and obeyed.

CONSCIENCES GOOD AND BAD

Granted that there is a moral order, how may we find the goalposts, discover the conditions that determine our life's meaning, the moral principles that are in the nature of things, and learn how to apply them?

103

Surely it is not easy. We are confused by thousands of wiseacres who know it all: parents, leaders in government and business and in the church say, "This is the way." Parents often are so dogmatic that they don't take the time to help their children find the "because-therefore." Discipline is always valuable when administered out of love and the "because . . . therefore" is explained. No matter how old we are, we need to listen to others; but in the final analysis each of us must find his own answers and not be taken in by the dogmatics of any person or system, whether it be the Democratic or Republican party, or Marxists, or the playboy society, or rigid Christian moralists.

Fortunately there is an innate resistance within each of us to being forced into any mold. We are free persons, and part of the structure of our freedom is what we call "conscience."

Conscience may be defined as that part of our thinking, willing, understanding mind that enables us to discriminate and to make choices. Conscience is that within us creating feelings of guilt or the opposite feelings of harmony and joy. The feelings of guilt are the warnings of a "bad conscience" and the feelings of harmony and joy are the rewards of a "good conscience." Guilt feelings are as necessary to finding the goalposts as pain reactions to learning the right and wrong ways of handling fire, and so forth.

Obviously, there is a false guilt and a true guilt, a sick conscience and a healthy conscience. The false guilt coming from a sick conscience is destructive indeed. The business of the psychiatrist, says Martin Buber, is to help the person feel guilty about what he should feel guilt about, and to remove the false guilt related to things he should not feel guilty about.

104

This, indeed, is the business of us all if we would help others; but we need to begin with ourselves.

There are six major desires or paths through which our consciences become either twisted and sick or healthy and right:

(a) the desire to be pleasing to others;

(b) the desire to enjoy my self (pleasures of narcissism);

(c) the desire to be superior to others;

(d) the desire to be perfect;

(e) the desire to use others;

(f) the desire to be united and in harmony with others.

These desires are always colliding and opposing each other. Let us see how true and false guilt are created in each of these ways.

The *desire to be pleasing to others* is very important in the early training of our consciences. Freud began a great new advance in psychotherapy by pointing up the influence of parents and other social restraints that begin back in early childhood. Feelings of guilt arise when parents scold us or the gang makes fun of us and we are afraid of their displeasure. Since we desire their approval we decide our goals and actions by saying, "Because to do this (or not to do this) will bring disfavor, therefore I will (or I will not) do it." My goals are decided by what is pleasing or displeasing to those I want to love me. This is a valuable way to learn as children. By the time we are five years old, we have learned more than we will in the next fifty years and much of it is by this pleasure-displeasure method. But as Freud points out, if this method of deciding my goals is carried over into adulthood, I am possessed and

105

motivated by an infantile guilt that may cripple me emotionally for life.

For instance, says Freud, we are imprisoned by taboos created by our early training. Sex may be considered taboo because of family teaching and example. A boy or a girl may grow up and marry but be unable to respond to each other sexually because of fear of breaking the taboo which resides in the subconscious mind. Since this is hurtful, Freud's answer is to get rid of all taboos. But then the person rebelling at all social restraint loses the belonging and the loving security he needs—we know something is wrong with such a goal also.

Since another strong desire is for our own pleasure, repression, not license, is considered by many the great evil and sexual matters are relegated to the realm of modern science instead of morals. Much of modern "right and wrong" is built on this goal. Pleasure becomes "the universal port of destination" as one modern pornographic novel declares and "every wind that blows thither" is a good one, provided no one gets hurt. This is one modern philosophy: Anything that is pleasurable is good—anything that denies pleasure is bad.[7]

But how do you decide whether a premarital sex adventure is going to produce harm or whether it is right and good? Can true love and its harmony and joy exist only outside marriage as the cult of romantic passion declares? Or can true love exist only where there is mutual reverence and respect and the ability to care responsibly for each other? With faithfulness in marriage, not only of the letter but of the spirit—isn't this the way finest harmony comes? How do you know?

One thing is sure, we will not find the answer simply by asking the question, "What will be pleasing to those whose love I need?" Nor will it be decided by the opposite reaction, "What will be pleasing to me sexually?" Either way I am in a blind alley, a slave to what others think or to my own craving for pleasure which cannot be satisfied.

There is another desire which according to Alfred Adler is the strongest of all: *the desire to be superior*, a desire made strong by the fear of being inferior. I feel guilty because I have failed to prove my superiority. I want to be a "number-one success." Because I am not Number One, therefore I am a failure. Because I have failed, I feel guilty; and my guilt feelings lead to hatred of myself and others, to bitterness, anxiety, envy, jealousy—perhaps to alcoholism, dope addiction, or to compulsive eating, smoking, even working. Certainly there are millions of people today who suffer greatly because of this false guilt. For they are using the wrong goalposts. Success measured in terms of rank and not in the fulfillment of our true selves or in creative accomplishment is certainly a false goal. Only a very few can be on top, and even they are always afraid of losing their position!

There is a fourth desire which can produce either true or false guilt when it is frustrated: *We all desire to be perfect*, at least in our own picture of perfection. Hence we cannot accept the "shadow-self" as C. J. Jung calls it. The shadow-self is the unpleasing part of ourselves and all of us have it. None of us can be perfect as we think we ought to be.

We are forever restless, dissatisfied, wanting to know everything, to do everything, to conquer everything. The grandeur and misery of man is in the way he meets his longing for perfection and what he does with his shadow-self, the constantly

107

recurring imperfection and the guilt and self-disgust because of it.

> A man's reach should exceed his grasp,
> Or what's a heaven for?

asks Robert Browning in "Andrea del Sarto." But when our grasp does not come near to our longing reach we are also likely to be in hell!

How much of our entertainment industry—the billions of dollars and millions of lives spent in escapist movies, alcohol, tobacco, food, and as male and female Don Juans—is an attempt to get rid of the "shadow-self"? There is a true self, but I cannot accept it because of the "shadow-self" which gets in the way.

There is also *the desire to use others to achieve any one of the other drives:* to prove that I am superior, to make me forget my shadow-self, to prove to me that I am lovable. This, says Martin Buber, is to have an "I-It" relationship rather than an "I-Thou." To treat another person as a thing is the meaning of lust. It also provides the reason for lying, stealing, and killing, whether in small uncaring ways or in sudden brutal cruelty. "I do this because you are a thing to be used to prove my point or to satisfy my pleasure or my egomania." Always, of course, when we treat other people as things, we have a real sense of guilt, which, added to the guilt of imperfection and failure we already have, drives us further and further away from the true goalposts of life. It is in this area we must look to find the reason for deciding on the right and wrong of certain acts such as sexual promiscuity, overeating, racial injustice, the use of alcohol, and the way we search for wealth and power.

A sixth basic desire has untold possibilities for helping us discover the real goalposts of life: *the desire to be united with others* in a true harmony of spirit. Omar Khayyam's classic words typify this desire:

> A Jug of Wine, a Loaf of Bread—and Thou
> Beside me singing in the Wilderness—
> Oh, Wilderness were Paradise enow![8]

We are made for community. "No man is an Island, entire of itself; every man is . . . a part of the main." [9] But here again, this desire to be united with others may lead to a pandering to their desires, an almost doglike desire to please, so that we are again in chains and lose the true goal of life.

The great problem of our human consciences is to find the way to keep all six of these desires in their proper perspective so that they are united in one great desire that adequately represents the central goal of life. Here alone a great faith in God as revealed in Christ is best able to provide the spirit and the method by which such unity is achieved. All six of these desires are good within limits and may lead us to a good conscience; and yet each of the six is destructive if taken as the final meaning of life. Let me illustrate:

"Because the family, the party, the gang, the company says it is necessary and right; therefore it is right—I make it my goal."

"Because money is necessary to be superior, therefore anything for money."

"Because I cannot accept my shadow-self—my unpleasing

109

looks, thoughts, appearance—therefore I am entitled to escape in drink, or excitement, or by acquiring power over others."

"Because I must be free to enjoy myself"; or

"Because others say it is my duty (to my country, my family, my group) I will treat others as things—anything to keep the approval of others." These are a few of the false goal-posts that produce the sense of guilt with which so many are ridden today. No wonder this century has been called "the century of the bad conscience" as contrasted with the so-called "good conscience [of the nineteenth century] we find shocking." [10]

The most hopeful possibility of finding life's true goals with an adequate set of "because-therefores" is through the use of all six of these desires as our consciences are made sensitive by our openness to the truth of God—a commitment to the mind of Christ. We need all that our parents and those who have gone before can teach us and the constraints of society up to a certain point. Certainly, the repression of all sex desires is unnatural and harmful. On the other hand, their complete and unbridled expression can be just as unnatural and harmful. We do need to be ambitious for our best possible creativity and self-fulfillment; but life is not a game where the superior always wins. The true success is one who uses what he has—one, two, or ten talents—in the most creative way. We certainly must accept ourselves, including the shadow-self which we do not like. We must learn to accept ourselves with all our imperfections and we must be sure that we are in right relationships with others. But each and all of these desires without the guidance of the Spirit of God in Christ may give us a false and twisted conscience.

110

SINAI REVISITED

How do we get a good conscience before God—that is, before Reality? "Listen to God" is the counsel of the prophets and our Lord, and others who have found the way. How do we "listen to God"?

We listen as we seek to understand the wisdom of the ages. Some of this wisdom comes through parents and friends. Some of it through great books of recent as well as ancient times. Much of it comes through the Bible, which, as no other book, is filled with the experiences of man and his quest for God and his purposes. Much of this wisdom is found in the testimony of human experience which reveals the laws or conditions of life that have been written in much suffering.

The principles thus discovered through the centuries remain constant, but our understanding of their application needs to be continually revised and applied to our present circumstances. For instance, the Ten Commandments formed the earliest summary of these constant principles or conditions of the good life. They are as appropriate today as in that ancient time, but their application is much different. The law against killing and stealing, for instance, was relatively a simple matter compared to our day when there are so many ways in which, knowingly or not, we participate in wholesale killings and theft. Perhaps the significance of these principles may be seen more clearly if they are stated positively rather than negatively in the light of present experience:

1. Put God first—that is, recognize yourself as a creature-child and not the Creator. You did not make the laws, God did. Be humble and open and obedient.

2. There are no substitutes for God—cast out every idol; that is, any good which you seek to make ultimate is an idol and always becomes evil.

3. Accept life's rhythms of rest and work, worship and rest.

4. Preserve your integrity—the necessity for faithfulness in relationship with God.

5. Reverence human life—there are hundreds of ways to kill. Remember the Lord of the Universe backs those who reverence the lives of others.

6. Observe the disciplines of the home and society when they bring freedom within just limits.

7. Respect others as well as yourself as persons and not things.

8. Tell the truth in love, always being true to the highest good for all.

9. Desires are not to be eliminated or indulged indiscriminately, but directed and controlled toward the one desire that sets us free: God's will.

10. Recognize the stewardship of possessions—all is given to us in trust for the well-being of all God's children.

Obviously, any such statement of the Ten Commandments interprets these basic conditions for the good life in the light of all human experience, which includes two thousand years of Christian history. As Christians we see these commandments in the light of the grace of God as revealed in Jesus Christ.

The most important "because-therefore" is written in John 3:16: "[Because] God so loved the world . . . he gave his only Son . . . [therefore] whoever believes in him should not perish but have eternal life." And its equally important corollary: "Because God so loved us, therefore we ought to love one another." We have not only Jesus, but Francis of Assisi, Albert Schweitzer and his "Reverence for Life," Martin Buber and his "I-Thou" relationship, and countless others. We have the insights in psychology and sociology which throw light on these basic conditions. If we are open before the truth, we will learn all we possibly can from others.

If we would find the goalposts for our day, however, we must not be bound by what the past has said. We need to respect the past and learn from it, but

> New occasions teach new duties,
> Time makes ancient good uncouth;
> They must upward still and onward,
> Who would keep abreast of truth.[11]

The specific goalposts have to be discovered in every situation. We must seek the true goal in each hour, each day; but the ultimate goals are always before us, shining like the sun.

For those of us who see reality in the face of Jesus Christ, Christlike love is the norm for true morality. The kind, wise, positive, strong love that was in Christ is the best test of what is right and wrong. But this love is not "eros" (possessing, desiring love) but "agape" (giving, caring, responsible love) which is "both absolute and relative by its very nature. An unchanging principle, it nevertheless always changes in its concrete application. It 'listens' to the particular situation." [12]

Life's goalposts are found by accepting ourselves and others as loved by God, including the shadow-self with all its imperfections. Thus we find the ability to move into a love for others that includes justice with mercy, a "creative justice." The goalposts are the loving purposes of God for me and all my brothers. Sometimes these purposes are easier to find than at other times; but they are always there. Faith in God as revealed in Christ makes me open, resilient, strong, and wise to say:

Because I have been loved, forgiven, and offered a new chance and the help I need to accept it; therefore I will love and forgive, offer to others a new chance and the help I can give them.

Because I am not treated as a thing by my Creator, therefore I will not treat others as things to be used for my own satisfaction, whether I am considering the wise use of sex or money or talent or vocational opportunity. In this spirit I never fail to find a "because-therefore" that brings meaning and assurance to my life.

"Any one who does not have the Spirit of Christ does not belong to him" (Rom 8:9), said Paul. Test the spirits—the desires that seek to determine what is right and wrong—by the Spirit of Christ. Get well acquainted with him through a study of the Gospels. Get to know him in the lives of others and in your own prayer and meditation. Then he will say to you, "Because you have kept my word of patient endurance, therefore I will keep you in the hour of trial."

HOPE and the
COURAGE to LIVE

The one thing lacking in modern man with all his magnificent scientific and material progress is the faith in the present and the future that enables him to live with hope and courage and sets him free to care responsibly for his fellows.

He has plenty of hope for a new scientific breakthrough which he has been led to expect with increasing frequency. But he often lacks the hope and the courage to live at his best in the face of the worst. Without hope, responsible love is unlikely if not impossible. Without hope, courage fails and we give up or settle for a way of escape that is shamefully destructive of our true responsibilities. Real tragedy always strikes when hope begins to die.

Certainly there are many things in our lives and world to cause discouragement. Every morning we pick up the paper and are dashed with a shower of cold water: A great leader of business or government commits suicide. Several children are killed by a bomb in a church during a race riot. Thousands of others are injured in body and mind. Thousands of youth are in despair leading to juvenile delinquency, which sociologists say is rebellion against the meaninglessness and rejection they have experienced.

The despair of millions in America and around the world after two wars which were to make the world safe for freedom are now finding less freedom than ever and the very existence of mankind threatened by atomic destruction! Such despair is the most dangerous single factor in the present, for it cuts the root of courageous and intelligent action.

What's the use of sacrificing and creative work, when all these have laid down their lives in vain? Why not get all you can while the getting is good, and forget the meaninglessness?

Camus said, "When life has no hopeful meaning, it becomes an exile . . . deprived of the memory of a lost home or the hope of a promised land."

Despair—the lack of hope—is the one thing most to be dreaded in human life. It is the root of suicide, murder, war, many accidents, and vast suffering. Charles Péguy, French poet who lost his life in World War I, wrote his conviction that we need all three virtues, faith, hope, and charity; but he points to the basic need for hope:

Faith is a great tree, an oak rooted in the heart of France.
And under the wings of that tree, Charity, my daughter
    Charity shelters all the woes of the world.
And my little hope is nothing but that little earnest of
    a bud which shows itself at the beginning of April . . .

And yet it is from that bud, on the contrary, that everything
comes. . . .
Without that one little budding of hope . . . the whole of my creation would be nothing but dead wood. And the dead wood will be
cast into the fire.
And my whole creation would be nothing than a huge cemetery.[1]

Two old sayings represent this great need: "Stay with it until
the cows come home!" "Hang on till hell freezes over!" Both
of these sayings represent the attitude of determined faith
which characterizes man at his best in the dark and difficult
hours of life.

The saying, "Until the cows come home," obviously origi-
nated in the country. Anyone familiar with milk cows knows
that sooner or later they do come home—to be fed and milked.
The saying indicates the confidence that there will be in the
future a better event than the present. The determination to
"wait until the cows come home" means to stay with it until
good times arrive. The second saying, "Till hell freezes over,"
represents the opposite, a very unlikely event. If I hang on till
this happens, I will never give up!

"Until" is the one word in common in all the biographies of
victorious men and women who have had the persistence and
the courage to see life through to the end and to turn life's
darkest hours into life's finest hours.

"When you get in a tight place, till it seems as though you
couldn't hold on a minute longer," wrote Harriet Beecher
Stowe, who had her share of dark hours, "never give up then;
for that is just the time and place that the tide will turn."

The ability to hold on until the tide turns, until the cows
come home and hell freezes over depends on our faith in the

future; and this depends on what we believe and on our willingness to bet our lives upon our belief concerning the reality that undergirds the present and the future. For Christians it is faith in the living God and Father of our Lord Jesus Christ—the conviction that underneath are the "Everlasting Arms." This phrase is also a symbolic expression of the nature of reality.

TWO VIEWS OF THE FUTURE

There are two different kinds of "until," representing two approaches to the future:

First, a *frustrated, but dogged* "*until.*" This approach says that history, social and personal, is a circle repeating itself. All ancient religions before the Hebrew Christian era taught this, as do most Eastern religions today. Some historians, including Arnold Toynbee, teach the circle theory of history: Nations, civilizations, and peoples rise, decay, and fall. Buddhism teaches the circle theory of human life—from one reincarnation to another, unless through great discipline one escapes the circle into Nirvana through union with the All.

"Apes and men go singularly back to the same dust." Many people today have this approach to their future: Human life in general and mine in particular is going nowhere. Life and history are a squirrel cage and we are the squirrels. Why hang on? The answer of the agnostic naturalists of today and the stoics in ancient Greece and Rome to this question is: Because it is our nature to hang on rather than to give up. Grit your teeth and stand it as long as you can. Yet, when things get too tough, suicide is really the noble way out. So Seneca and many "noble" Romans committed suicide, as some people do today.

In the same way the Japanese "hara-kiri" was considered to be the honorable way out of dark hours.

Why hang on when the going is tough, since it is heroic to take one's life? Lucan, the Roman philosopher, answers, "Man's best lot is to know how to die, and the next best is to be compelled to." For as Seneca says, "Death means only not to be."

What a difference the Christian approach to the future makes: The future, as the present, is under the rule of the Living God. It is not a dreary circle or a lonely journey into nothingness. But for those who love and trust God the future is a growing, a becoming, through all the pains and struggles, to a triumphant fulfillment! Faith in the God of Christ still gives to those committed to it hope for the future and the courage to be and live in spite of all life's threats and discouragement. Can this statement be validated in experience? I think it can.

"We are saved by hope." Thus Paul declares the facts of human life. "But if we hope for what we do not see, we wait for it with patience" (Rom. 8:24-25). And Martin Luther declared, "Everything that is done in the world is done in hope."

Hope is the attitude of eager expectation: the confident look to the future as having possibilities unrealized in the present. In the Greek legend of Pandora's Box, the curious girl opened the lid in spite of repeated warnings and let out all the troubles and evils that afflict mankind. As Hesiod tells the story he remarks that only Hope remained in the box. Psychiatrist Karl Menninger says this is still the source of human misery: "Hope stays there, cowering and crouching too much of the time."

He points out that our libraries hold many books on the importance of faith and love, but not one single volume had he been able to find on hope. *The Encyclopaedia Britannica* devotes many columns to the topic of love and faith, but "poor little hope . . . is not even listed." Menninger concludes that "the best thing a psychiatrist can do for his patients is to light them a candle of hope to show them the possibilities that may become sound expectations."

THE SOURCE OF HOPE

How do we light a candle of hope for ourselves and others and for all mankind so that we find eager expectations of possibilities to come? How do we get the courage to hang on till hell freezes over and the cows come home?

There are only two possible sources: either from ourselves or from a source infinitely greater than we whom we call God. There are still many persistent humanists today with what might be termed a cheery optimism, who bid us to live hopefully and courageously by depending on no God higher than that within ourselves.

There are two kinds of atheists: those who say they do not believe in God and those who act as if they didn't, though they say they do. Modern men, including many professing Christians, obviously are practicing, if not professing, atheists who really place their hope in themselves, their smartness, their ingenuity, and their own resources. Is this an adequate source of hope?

The test comes when we find ourselves up against the sad and often tragic absurdities of life. Albert Camus, in *The Myth* of *Sisyphus*, interprets another old Greek legend about the man who was punished by the gods for the remainder of his life by being compelled to push a huge rock up the mountainside. Just when he got the rock to the top, the rock always would come crashing down again and he had to start the dreary process all over again. This is the way life is, says Camus. In order to have any courage at all you accept the absurdities of life. You choose to get all the good you can in the moment of existence. Eat, drink, be merry, or do whatever you think is good, for tomorrow you die. Or else you reject the absurdity of existence when things get too tough, and get out of it as painlessly as possible.

And yet, if I am nothing but a pitiable Sisyphus senselessly rolling a rock up the mountain, knowing it will roll back down again, how can I have hope, not only to hang on for another five minutes, but to be eagerly expectant of good possibilities? How can I be hopeful in an evil and dangerous old world in the face of coming world destruction, or at least of old age and death? This is an insurmountable problem for anyone without a living faith in God.

The agnostic humanists answer: Hope in yourself, your resiliency, your own intelligent power to wrest good even out of such senseless evil. With William Ernest Henley they urge us to cry,

> In the fell clutch of circumstance
> I have not winced nor cried aloud.
> Under the bludgeonings of chance
> My head is bloody, but unbowed.

. . . .

121

It matters not how strait the gate,
  How charged with punishments the scroll,
I am the master of my fate;
  I am the captain of my soul.[2]

This all sounds very noble; but what happens when the worst is too much to take, as it surely does become, and there is nothing but absurdity left? If I am alone on the cross, I will someday give up in despair.

Millions do just that: cracking up emotionally, mentally, morally—with suicides, bitterness, despair! A long way from the vital, joyous, triumphant experience of vital Christians in every age.

Look what happened to some of the finest humanists of recent history who refused to believe in God. They all began with high hopes that man was on an escalator of progress going up all the time; but within a span of fifty years they repudiated their earlier hope.

George Bernard Shaw in "Back to Methuselah" wrote, "I have no hope for man. He is going to commit suicide; but have no fear, another species will arise and everything will go on."

Such a despairing attitude certainly strips the last vestige of expectation that might inspire man to work for peace, though strangely enough Shaw contradicted himself by leading demonstrations to "ban the bomb." Perhaps he had more faith than he professed, and therefore some real hope.

H. G. Wells also finally despaired of man. Feeling that the universe was bored with its most bothersome inhabitant, he wrote, "Mankind, which began in a cave and behind a windbreak, will end in the disease soaked ruins of a slum."

And Clarence Darrow, champion of the underdog, wrote, "Emotionally I exist, with my last breath I shall probably try to draw another. But life is such a welter and play of inscrutable forces, that no thinking, humane person would inflict it on another."

We admire their nobility and determination to stick with it without hope; but as we listen to these finest examples of those who look for hope in their own wisdom and strength, we are reminded of the words of Paul speaking of those who are "without God and without hope in the world." Obviously the two go together: In the long run to be without God is indeed to be without hope in the world.

Indeed, hope for the atheist, and in the long run, for the agnostic humanist, is the enemy. The Greeks left hope out of their philosophy on purpose because they believed in an unshakable fate, and therefore hope was an illusion. Hope causes you to have expectations that will be disappointed; therefore it is better not to hope. Aeschylus spoke of hope as "the food of exiles," and Euripides described it as "man's curse." The same attitude is found in modern man. Nietzsche declared hope to be the worst of evils because it prolonged the pain of mankind.

Surely the evidence is overwhelming that without faith in a living God whose purposes are written into the very nature of all the universe, there is no hope worth the name. The courage to hang on till the end is only a dogged but absurd determination of those who for the time being would rather hang on than give up.

What a different climate we meet in the Bible. The ancient psalmist faced with all the evils of man cried,

> Hope in God; for I shall yet praise him,
> my help and my God (Ps. 42:11).

And one of Paul's great prayers reads, "Now the God of hope fill you with all joy and peace in believing, that ye may abound in hope, through the power of the Holy Ghost" (Rom. 15:13, KJV).

Who is God? God is the Lord of hope—the source and ground of hope without which life at best is impossible. "The creation was subjected to futility [absurdity], not of its own will but by the will of him who subjected it in hope" (Rom. 8:20).

The God back of, underneath, and in this vast universe is a God of eager expectations. He foresees vast possibilities for his universe and for his chosen family; for we are his children, heirs of his eager expectations and infinite resources, and fellow heirs with Christ, who taught us to pray:

> Thy kingdom come,
> Thy will be done,
> On earth as it is in heaven.

Since God the Almighty Creator, Ruler, Father of all is the God of hope, his Spirit will fill you with all joy and peace in believing so that you may be overflowing with the same eager expectation that has brought all things into being! This is the meaning of Paul's faith.

Therefore the New Testament and the prophets in the Old Testament and the great spirits in every age since would declare: There are no hopeless situations. There are only men without hope. One of the early Christian fathers, Clement of

124

Alexandria, spoke of hope as the lifeblood of faith: "When hope expires, it is as if the blood flowed forth and the vitality of faith is destroyed." [3]

This was what had happened to the ancient world in which Paul lived and spoke, what historians call "loss of nerve," the lifeblood of faith, was gone. But the faith of the Christians in Christ as Lord revealing the God of hope brought a new hope into that ancient world. The ancient *Letter to Diognetus* describes this faith and its results: "This new . . . way of life [eager concern] has appeared on earth now and not earlier." [4]

Lecky, the historian, writes of the early church, "There sprang a stern, aggressive and at the same time disciplined enthusiasm wholly unlike any other that had been witnessed upon the earth." It was this "disciplined enthusiasm" which helped produce the Renaissance and the Age of Science. It is too bad we take the results and forget the cause.

WHEN FAITH CONQUERS DESPAIR

Look at the difference today that faith in the God of hope revealed in Christ makes in our power to hope. Consider the three major human conflicts that bring despair:

First, consider *the conflict with our circumstances* of inheritance and environment that without the God of hope inevitably lead to discouragement and despair.

This conflict is especially felt in our youth, but extends even to old age. Of course, some few people are buttressed with a great family background, a famous name, or a large fortune. But no matter how good our family or how large our inheritance, every human being has to struggle with the absurd demands of his or her situation. If I do not have to struggle for money I may have a conflict with some bodily or mental handicap: A girl with wealth and position but a homely face; a boy with a brilliant I.Q., but with a weak physical constitution; a Jimmy Durante with a huge nose. I may have a highly sensitive nervous system. Perhaps my parents were immature or self-centered. Suppose my father is an alcoholic, or my mother loose in morals. Maybe they are well intentioned but unwisely may do those things that leave me feeling rejected, unwanted, and unimportant. Or perhaps my wife or my husband does not understand me and thwarts and opposes me at every turn, leaving my ego battered, if not shattered! These are some of the kinds of conflicts we all have in one form or another. We can't get out of them any more than we can jump out of our skins.

How often a person is on the edge of despair because his situation seems hopeless—he can't change the circumstances. The older we get, the worse our discouragements become. We are all faced with the basic question, as Hamlet is,

> To be or not to be: that is the question:
> Whether 'tis nobler in the mind to suffer
> The slings and arrows of outrageous fortune,
> Or to take arms against a sea of troubles,
> And by opposing end them? [5]

There is a third alternative which the true Christian possesses: He may be saved in hope: the girl with too small a nose or with buckteeth may grow up to be beloved and honored in spite of the handicap. Jimmy Durante makes capital of his big nose and those who know him best love him as a beautiful person. Helen Keller, blind, deaf, and dumb, found hope through the love of Anne Sullivan because she found meaning in everything: first water, then the trees, her family, love, and then God. When Phillips Brooks, the great preacher, through Anne Sullivan told her of Christ, she said, "I have known him for a long, long, time; but I did not know his name." She had found Christ and hope in Anne Sullivan's love. Without the Christ in Anne Sullivan, Helen Keller would have given up in despair.

Yes, the name of God is hope: eager expectation looking to the vast possibilities in the present and future! Without this we cannot live well, in spite of all handicaps. With it we are able for anything!

Consider also the difference faith in the God of hope as revealed in Christ makes in *the conflicts caused by our roles in life*. This is especially difficult for adults. We are all caught in the role we must play in home, in business, or in our profession. There is on one hand what I expect, and on the other hand, what is expected of me. These are always in conflict to some extent, no matter how fine my home and my job may be. That is, I am expected to do some things I don't like and even hate doing. I can do one of three things:

(a) I can stay with my role, all the while resenting parts of it bitterly, silently, or explosively. I may fight it to my dying day and waste my joys and peace in anxious, resentful living.

(b) I can run away, find a new role, change jobs, get a new wife or husband. Every year millions of people try this method: They disappear, or divorce and remarry or change jobs—but they soon discover that the new role they have chosen also has its drawbacks and demands against which they rebel. In every job and every marriage there are expectations for me I will not

127

like. Sinclair Lewis' Babbitt, the successful businessman from Main Street in Big Town, tried to run away to the Maine woods, but he soon discovered as we all do that "he could never run away from himself."

No, I can't go back to the Garden of Eden or to some paradisaical state, though as Sigmund Freud points out, this is what all of us at times try to do. All emotionally sick people try to go back to their mother's womb with its perfect security and freedom from all demands.

(c) Or I may be saved by hope in my present role through a commitment of faith in Christ so that I see in it not only the absurdities I don't like, but also a deeper role which the New Testament calls living as sons and daughters of God— brothers in the same family. Then I will do the hard and difficult thing with joy and victory.

Our hope is in believing that we are not alone in our struggles and in seeing a divine meaning to it all. As Paul says it, "The whole created universe groans in all its parts as if in the pangs of childbirth" (Rom. 8:22, NEB).

"Why should I have such struggles, such pains?" a mother might cry with her first pangs of childbirth. We say to her, "A baby is being born; hang on, with eager hope and expectations for its birth." She is filled with all joy and peace in believing that a baby is being brought to life. The more such hope she has, the easier and faster the birth.

This is what Paul is saying: We are God's sons; if we suffer with him, we may live with him. We are growing up into a priceless maturity of infinite value to God, to others, and to ourselves. "The whole creation is on tiptoe to see the wonderful sight of the sons of God coming into their own" (Rom. 8:19, Phillips).

Our role as God's children is magnificent in its development, which is small now. What I see of this new life is not much; but remember, "Hope that is seen is not hope. For who hopes for what he sees? But if we hope for what we do not see, we wait for it with patience" (Rom. 8:25). "The sufferings we now endure bear no comparison with the splendour, as yet unrevealed, which is in store for us" (Rom. 8:18, NEB).

CONQUEST OF MEANINGLESSNESS

What a difference the God of hope makes in our conflict with meaninglessness which otherwise leads to despair. Recently in one week three families in the church I served were faced with three separate accidents in which two fine young men and one mother were killed. In such a time even the finest philosophy of life is not enough to save us from despair. All of us will in some way or time face great suffering, accidents, disease, or death—and it all seems so utterly meaningless.

At such a time it is natural to cry, "Why does this have to happen to me and my dear one? What's the use? I can't go on!" And the simple truth is that without meaning we cannot and will not go on very long. We will either give way to rebellion and waste and destroy our opportunities in the present like a burning star that soon goes out; or we may try to pluck up our courage and accept the absurdities within our own meager resources. But how can we do so for long without some gleam of meaning, without some hope to hold us?

Only faith in the God of hope can open the doors of meaning and resulting hope for us—faith in the One who rules

129

now and forever in the Spirit of Christ, making even the wrath and evil of men to praise him—faith that good is coming and therefore I am going, eagerly, expectantly, out to meet it!

Part of the meaning we see is in the fact of freedom. Much of the evil and suffering in our world is the price we pay for freedom, a freedom within the limits of a universe ruled by the God of love and justice. Two facts cannot be denied, as seen from our human experience: (a) Growth of intelligence, insight, and creative powers come through struggle which we meet with faith and obedience. The frailty and freedom that provide the struggle seem necessary for our growth. (b) Degeneration, disease, weakness, and much useless and unnecessary suffering are the result of our failure to obey the laws of our being. This we considered in the preceding chapter. Whatever we believe about chance or predestination we cannot ignore the tremendous fact of human freedom.

"I demand the right to be damned," Gilbert K. Chesterton insisted. Why? Because if we are to have a world that gives us Jesus, Beethoven, Raphael, and Michelangelo, we must accept a world where a Nero, a Napoleon, or a Hitler are also possible. Therefore the right to be damned is a priceless right, for it points to the moral and spiritual structure that men may ignore at their peril. As the Greek, Aeschylus, said a long time ago, "Suffering is education." Whether it is learning that fire burns or that hatred and selfishness hurt and destroy, this is evidence of the pedagogical value of suffering. To say that all this is by chance is the most absurd, irrational of all positions one can take. We may learn, as did Shakespeare's Regan, who said, concerning King Lear's suffering,

O, sir, to wilful men,
The injuries that they themselves procure
Must be their schoolmasters.[6]

Of this I am sure: much of the evil and suffering we endure is our schoolmaster to teach and discipline us as sons—if we are willing to learn!

This we can understand, but what about natural catastrophies, such as disease, insanity, floods, earthquakes? How can this have meaning? Here again we cannot see all the answers, but the fact of growth through struggle and pain is part of the meaning we can see.

Knowledge by suffering entereth,
And life is perfected by death.[7]

This we believe. "The whole creation has been groaning in travail together until now . . . [waiting] for the redemption of our bodies . . . [till we] obtain the glorious liberty of the children of God" (Rom. 8:22, 21). How do you know? Here is another pointer—a dependable law of life that says any situation with possibilities of life and growth also has possibilities of hurt and injury.

Perhaps this is the reason God made flies and mosquitos, sparrows and bugs. As a boy I spent hours wondering about this. I think it bothered me more than the great tragedies. I just could not understand why on earth a good, sensible God would make a flea! Suppose you decide to play God and destroy all the sparrows, as the little human gods in certain parts of America did. Soon you find out you are not as smart as you thought, for then hordes of insects come to eat up the crops.

It seems that nature has a balance which must not be upset. We must endure even flies and sparrows and snakes for a reason.

Night Flight,[8] by Antoine de Saint-Exupery, is a parable of our lives. It is the account of the early days of aviation when the international mails were trusted to the small, vulnerable planes, without the modern instruments we know today. The pilots and wireless operators were called on to make night flights without beacons and radio directional beams and radar which we think are so necessary. With a compass and the stars they set out across deserts and mountains.

The central character of the book is Riviere, manager of the company who had undertaken the business of flying the mails, and who is responsible for the entire service. He knows that airmail will perish if planes cannot fly in the dark, "for the lead we gain by day on ships and railways is lost each night." So with Riviere, "nothing matters but the end in view . . . . not that he wished to make slaves of men; his aim was to raise them above themselves."

One of the pilots was lost in a cyclone over the Patagonian desert. The book describes the suffering of his young wife of six months. Why did he have to die? In order that the mails might go through. Given the ultimate value of the goal, the sacrifices and the discipline have meaning. But is the goal of getting the mail through worth the life of one pilot? Does Riviere have a right to send the pilots out? Hence the deeper question arises. All of life is like a night flight. If the end is the development of sons of God, the development of that which is worthy, which lifts mankind's vision and endures forever, then the sacrifices of human life and all the costs in suffering are worth it. The New Testament declares that it is infinitely worth it. To paraphrase its teaching concerning suffering: God does not let us suffer to make slaves of us, but to raise us above ourselves to develop our highest powers. Therefore the sacrifice of his Son on the cross was worth it, for he is the pioneer and leader of our salvation. In tasting death he should stand for us all. (See also Hebrews 5:7-10.)

There is an old legend of the time when birds hopped contentedly around on the ground with their tiny legs, pecking here and there for food. One day God visited them and put two wings on each bird. How they did complain! They fussed and were irritable about this useless, extra burden, so unjust and unnecessary. Then one day one of the silly birds stretched his wings and began to flap them and found to his amazement that by their use he could lift himself off the ground. So it was that the birds found their burdens necessary in order to receive the power to fly! Certainly this is a parable of all life.

The whole question is: What is our destiny? To be contented cows or sons of God? Is there an eternal destiny that lifts us above all the misery and suffering; or just when we begin to live, do we die and that is all? No! This is not all! "The whole creation is on tiptoe to see . . . the sons of God coming into their own" (Rom. 8:18, Phillips). If this is so, as experience seems to declare, we can believe that underneath the burdens are wings, and underneath the suffering is growth, and underneath the tragedy is the greater victory. Our eternal destiny lifts us above all our misery and suffering, even death.

Remove the natural evils that cause such suffering—take away all struggle with cold and hunger, storms and disease and death, and we would be nothing but flabby jellyfish, with no

133

character. We would be deprived of the noblest and highest in life: helpfulness, compassion, courage, pity, love would be lost. But if we are sons of God coming into our own through suffering made adequate in trials, then we can "rejoice in [our sufferings because of] our hope of sharing the glory of God" (Rom. 5:2).

Surely Henry Suso was right when he said, "Suffering is the ancient law of love; there is no quest without pain, there is no lover who is not also a martyr." And if God himself suffers with us, as the cross declares, so with our Lord we too may be made fully adequate for our great destiny with the suffering we must endure. Therefore we must try and fail and try again, each time arising with "half of a broken hope for a pillow at night," but with the understanding that right will prevail, that "the smooth will bloom from the rough"—and this must be enough.

We are not alone.

Whether or not the smooth will bloom from the rough depends on the ultimate nature of reality—that is, upon God. Without a living faith in the God whose nature is revealed in the victory of his Son, there isn't any ground for hopeful meaning.

"Where is your carpenter now?" one of the Roman gladiators is said to have asked a Christian condemned to die in the arena. Without hesitation he answered, "He is making a coffin for your emperor." Undoubtedly this was the kind of deathless confidence that held the early Christians and that has made the Christian faith, when it has been genuine, the most powerfully hopeful faith known to man.

Sir Winston Churchill met with his cabinet on the morning after France capitulated. It was Britain's darkest hour—she was alone. After he had finished speaking he looked at his ministers. He saw despair written on most of their faces. Some were ready to give up. Then Churchill said, "Gentlemen, we are all alone, and I find it very exhilarating." He had hope—eager expectation of vast possibilities yet untouched.

So we may face our world at war, the evils and tragedies of our personal and social conflicts. If we accept the power for hope as the gift of the God of hope, we too may find this rather inspiring than despairing. This can be our finest hour. Why? Because God is the God of absurdity? No; but because God is the God of hope. We can say, "If God is for us, who is against us?"

Because I believe in the God of hope, I must say with William Faulkner, "I decline to accept the end of man. . . . I believe that man will not merely endure: he will prevail. He is immortal, not because he alone among creatures has an inexhaustible voice, but because he has a soul, a spirit capable of compassion and sacrifice and endurance." [9]

Faulkner might not have credited his hope to any articulate faith in God but as for me I believe this, because I believe in the God of hope who with eager expectancy over billions of years created this earth and billions more planets and suns—and called me to live as his son with endless resources which nothing can destroy.

Because I place my hope in the God of hope revealed in Christ and in those who have caught his Spirit, therefore I say with William Wordsworth,

Enough, if something from our hands have power
To live, and act, and serve the future hour;
And if, as toward the silent tomb we go,
Through love, through hope, and faith's transcendent dower,
We feel that we are greater than we know.[10]

LIFE in
DEATH

Life is filled with absurdities—some wonderful, even beautiful, some funny, some tragic. Belief in the resurrection of Christ might be called one of the disturbingly beautiful absurdities that for millions of Christians in every century brings the best out of the worst, hope out of despair, joy out of sorrow, and life out of death. It is inconceivable to our staid, prosaic minds: the cries and tears of black Friday and Saturday with its deep tragedy; the alleluias and joy of Easter Sunday—and life is different from then on! Yet this is the experience to which many vital Christians in every land all over the world witness today as in every age. Of course, not all who come to church on Easter Sunday will experience this, by any means. For many there will be only the sound of the words and the music. They will see only the lilies, the lovely new Easter clothes and the crowds, and that's all.

137

The real Resurrection experience may be summed up in the words Jesus spoke to Mary and Martha, overcome by grief over the death of their brother, Lazarus: "I am the resurrection and I am life. If a man has faith in me, even though he die, he shall come to life; and no one who is alive and has faith shall ever die" (John 11:25-26, NEB).

This is the "good news" told by the New Testament—the story repeated in thousands of lives. The good news or "gospel" has its origin in the true life story of the noblest, the kindest, most loving man who ever lived, who was cruelly murdered, his body mutilated and laid in a borrowed tomb. John puts the tragic denouement of those three years of sunshine and hope, of inspiration together with their friend and Master thus: "So the disciples went home again; but Mary stood at the tomb outside, weeping" (John 20:10-11, NEB).

But the story is good news, for there is an unexpected ending to this deep human tragedy, the tragedy with which we are all too familiar:

She turned round and saw Jesus standing there, but did not recognize him. Jesus said to her, "Why are you weeping? Who is it you are looking for?" Thinking it was the gardener, she said, "If it is you, sir, who removed him, tell me where you have laid him, and I will take him away." Jesus said, "Mary!" (John 20:14-15, NEB.)

She could never forget that voice—no one but Jesus ever had said "Mary" like that! She turned to him and said with unutterable joy, " 'Rabbuni ... My Master.' " And she ran to the disciples with her news, "I have seen the Lord!" (See John 20:14-18, NEB.)

"Absurd!" some of you with what is called a rational, realistic approach to life are saying. "Surely you don't expect me to believe that. How perfectly absurd—a dead man coming back to life! It may be a lovely fairy story, a fanciful allegory, but nothing in it is sure and dependable for me in this atomic space age. The one thing I am sure of is death—maybe taxes—but after a man is dead, he does not come to life!" All of us have had similar doubts and they need to be faced. In this last chapter I do not want to argue with these doubts, though I have many times argued with such doubts in my own mind, without, I am afraid, doing much good.

Instead of arguing, I simply want to present certain facts of human experience and let them speak for themselves. I will not call them "proofs," for there is no proof conclusive that can convince a skeptical mind. But however one explains it, the Resurrection experience is a fact of human life.

It was a very real experience for the first Christians who were shocked and surprised to meet the Risen Lord, and some of them would not believe unless they had actually touched and examined the wounds left by the Crucifixion.

Very few historians question the authenticity of the account of Jesus' crucifixion and death. Nor do they question the fact that the disciples believed Christ to be alive. Upon this the whole New Testament gives common witness. The differences, of course, have to do with whether their account of the Resurrection was a factual, historical account or whether their experiences were subjective altogether.

Markus Barth, distinguished young New Testament scholar, son of the great theologian Karl Barth, declares that neither viewpoint can be "proved" by purely historical research.

Faith stands against faith on either side. . . . the arguments proffered to disprove the historicity of the resurrection are at least as dogmatically prejudiced and as fallible as the arguments to the contrary. For example, how can Rudolf Bultmann prove that on Easter morning nothing else happened, or was given by God, but the birth of Easter faith in some disciples? [1]

Many great Christian minds have believed with Barth that "the resurrection took place bodily and not symbolically . . . watched by men of flesh and blood, not fabricated by hallucination." [2]

Certainly, Barth is correct in saying that the New Testament witnesses speak as surely of the Resurrection as of the Crucifixion of their Lord. It was their experience of the Risen Lord that produced their courageous victory of love and creative self-giving. To believe that the mighty spiritual movement which has "turned the world upside down" and has left us all in debt was the result of a delusion or hallucination is perhaps the most absurd position a supposedly rational mind could take.

We must begin with the disciples' experience and the experience of countless others through the ages. In their confident faith in God who "raised him up, having loosed the pangs of death, because it was not possible for him to be held by it" (Acts 2:24), they were new creations in Christ filled with the fruits of the Spirit: love, joy, peace, gentleness, patience. Each one must interpret and decide for himself whether he believes the Resurrection experience is reality or illusion. Not until we have fulfilled the conditions in our own lives in wholehearted commitment and trust can we know one way or another.

But how can I have faith in that which I cannot understand? It seems to be true that most of our understandings come as a result of our experience and not always as a prelude to it. Faith in the resurrection of Christ is not so much unreasonable as beyond reason. When we experience what the disciples called the presence of the Living Christ, we do have many understandings that we could never have before and our reason is lighted as with a thousand candlepower light. The evidences that lead us to a faith commitment are reasonable— much more so than the absurdities of reason declaring for the acceptance of only that which can be understood. This latter approach to life would have prevented every scientific discovery as well as every personal victory in courageous living. When he was President of the United States Woodrow Wilson said,

My life would not be worth living if it were not for the driving power of religion, for *faith*, pure and simple. I have seen all my life the arguments against it without ever having been moved by them. . . . There are people who *believe* only so far as they *understand*—that seems to me presumptuous and sets their understanding as the standard of the universe . . . I am sorry for such people! [3]

Let us therefore begin with experience as we seek for understanding and commitment to the highest reality.

First, let us consider some other human absurdities connected with death, whose irrationality is so utterly foolish that the Resurrection story is reasonable indeed in comparison. Then let us hear the witness of those who have found the vantage point of the faith that enables them to see above the rough, serried peaks of these farcical human absurdities and

141

arrive at an experience that gives victory and joy to life—a fact of experience that illustrates Jesus' words, "He who believes in me . . . shall never die" (John 11:26).

THE HARD FACT OF DEATH

Consider first the tragic and utterly foolish absurdity of our human attitudes toward death as generally held from the time of the ancients until now.

Tolstoy's version of an old Asiatic tale illustrates this absurdity. A traveler in a wild country is attacked by wild beasts and takes refuge in a waterless well. But after he gets into the well he sees at the bottom a fierce dragon ready to devour him. The wild beasts are above and the dragon is below, and he is caught in between. So he catches on to the branch of a wild bush growing in a crevice in the wall. Though his arms are tired he holds on grimly. And then to his horror he notices two mice, one black and one white, nibbling their way around the root of the bush. He knows the root will soon break off and he will fall into the jaws of the dragon. Looking around he sees some drops of honey on the leaves of the bush. So he stretches out his tongue and licks the honey and for the moment forgets his precarious situation.[4]

So man is perched precariously over death. This is the worst absurdity of all—refusing to face the fact of death, thinking and acting as if we were immortal in our present state—sure that we are going to live forever—spending all our energy licking the honey on the plant, when at any moment the root will break. And just as we get "fixed" and ready to live, we die! How absurd!

Robert Ruark in *Poor No More* tells the story of a poor boy,

Craig Price, who determines at all cost to be a rich man. Succeeding beyond his wildest dreams in achieving great wealth, he refused to think of his mortality. His was a

superbly constructed body . . . a fortress—impregnable against cancer, a bastion against heart disease, solidly sound against all ills. Other people would get sick, but not Craig Price. Perhaps other people would die—he had stopped reading the New York World-Telegram sports pages because the obituaries of so many of his acquaintances were on the other side—but not Craig Price.[5]

But like the rest of us, Craig Price was able to forget death only so long. One day the fact of his mortality hit him—a pain in the chest—and he woke up in a London hospital.

How strange that the most sought after achievement of our times seems to be the ability to forget death altogether, to conceal it in work and play, in piling up money. When we die we may bury our dead under a mountain of flowers—and we continue up to the very last to lick the honey on the plant.

There are other more realistic persons who are determined to face the fact of death, but without Christ. That is, they either refuse to believe, or they believe with their lips but refuse to act on the faith that there is a God of love who gives meaning and value to human life so that death is not the end, but the beginning. "When you are dead, that's it!" How many professing Christians live as though they believe that. But what happens when we live merely to die and that is all.

The condemned man in Sartre's story, The Wall, was such an honest materialist. Spending the agonizing hours of his last night, he looked back to the years when he had given himself to good causes, trying to achieve something worthwhile taking everything seriously then, because he believed himself immortal. He did not mean "immortal" after death but in life —never having faced death in reality. But now there was nothing he could take seriously—love, friends, causes to which he once gave himself, or even the feelings of his condemned fellow prisoners. So he cried bitterly, that his life was worth nothing because it was finished.

As long as we cannot see death, we may give ourselves to causes, duties, achievements—just for the fun of it. But in the face of the fact of death all this comes to nothing. It all seems useless. It is hard to get worked up over virtues, duties, and achievements when after all you must die. Oh, you might do a little bit for those who come after you, but they are going to die also. The whole thing has the smell of death on it, and what does it matter anyway?

The finest answer of the so-called "honest realists" is no better than the answer of ancient Epicurus: "We can take precautions against all sorts of things; but so far as death is concerned, we all of us live like the inhabitants of a defenseless citadel. . . . we spend our lives in waiting and we are condemned to die."

So what do we do while we wait? Like the man in the well we stick out our tongues and get all the sweet out of life that we can. We enjoy ourselves in our defenseless citadel, keeping the necessary supply of bread and water, and as much meat and cake as we can. If we want to be kind and unselfish because it makes us feel better, fine; but there is no real point to it if we feel better being unkind. So without Christ and his resurrection, the conclusion of the book of Ecclesiastes in the Bible is still the best we can say: "For the fate of the sons of men and the fate of beasts is the same; as one dies, so dies the other. They all have the same breath, and man has no advantage over the beasts; for all is vanity" (Eccl. 3:19).

Life without Christ is a living death without hope. Indeed, if we do not believe in the Resurrection, hope is the enemy! So said the Epicureans, and so say the modern agnostics, for all our unhappiness springs from hope that tempts us and exposes us to disappointment in the expectation of salvation. But if there is no salvation, then "death is at the bottom of every evil passion. Pride, greed, ambition are deadly in their results. There is no other evil in the world except death." [6] Paul put it simply: "If in this life we who are in Christ have only hope, we are of all men most to be pitied" (I Cor. 15:19).

We may lick the honey off the plant that holds us up for a few minutes longer, but

> To and fro about the town
> The dead men hurry up and down;
>
> Whirling corpses, moving dust,
> Driven of gold and greed and lust,
>
> Filmy-eyed and gray of cheek,
> How they babble, bite and squeak!
>
> . . . .
>
> But these are dead men, with no thought
> Of things that are not sold or bought.
>
> . . . .
>
> In their bodies there is breath,
> But their souls are steeped in death.[7]

145

THE FACT OF GREAT LIFE IN DEATH

Thank God there is another level of human experience: The resurrected life by faith in Christ and his resurrection—the continuing miracle of those noble spirits who have overcome the absurdity of death by living the fullest, richest, and most worthwhile lives known to man!

How may we, like them, find the Great Life even in death?

First, certainly, *not by ignoring or trying to escape death.* "It is appointed to men once to die." Christians at their realistic best, like the agnostic existentialists of our day, know that we can live at our best only as we learn to face death. To do this does not require us to go to the extremes as did a certain group of monks during the Middle Ages. They insisted on living in the same room where the dead bodies of their comrades continued to be kept, whether in the stage of decay or after decay was ended and only the bones remained. You can visit their monastery today in Rome and see the way daily, hourly, momentarily they faced the fact of death.

We do not need to use such methods, but from Jesus to Paul, Augustine to Wesley, Christians have been taught that *you cannot begin to live until you have already died.* Obviously we are using the words "die" and "death" here in two different senses.

"He who believes in me, though he die, yet shall he live, and whoever lives and believes in me shall never die" (John 11:26). "I die every day" (I Cor. 15:31), wrote Paul. "I have been crucified with Christ; it is no longer I who live, but Christ who lives in me; and the life I now live in the flesh I live by faith in the Son of God, who loved me and gave himself for me" (Gal. 2:20).

The one who dies to the false life, with its pride and pretensions, will never die to the true life and even if he dies physically, he will come to life!

What a difference there is in death for one with Christ and one without him!

The agnostic or unbeliever facing death, unable any longer to ignore it, is likely to be very "self-conscious." He may also be conscious of those about him who love him; but since for him this is the end of everything he is rarely able to be truly concerned with anything much except his own disastrous journey into nothingness.

The Christian's dying is centered not in himself but in Christ and is almost completely "Christ" and "other-conscious." How many countless illustrations of this are found in the record of trusting Christians at the hour of their death. Susanna Wesley, mother of eighteen children, including John and Charles Wesley, in her last moments called her children and their families about her and said, "As soon as I am released, children, sing a psalm of praise to God." She was thinking of her friend, the Man of Sorrows, "who could not be held by the pangs of death." Her last words were for him only, and spoken in a tone of glad surprise: "My dear Saviour! Are you come to help me in my extremity at last?" [8] True, there have been some brave deaths among unbelievers—but nothing compared with the quality of this, or with her son John's famous last words, "The best of all is God is with us!"

Instead, we find appropriate Carl Sandburg's warning, "Beware the little deaths." Without faith in Christ's resurrection, we are often unable to overcome the little deaths of self-concern, whereby day by day we die, little by little. Compare

147

the bravest characters in ancient Rome or among modern agnostics. Compare the ordinary run-of-the-mill folk who live self-centered lives, wanting their own pleasure, security and exaltation above anything else with those who are alive in Christ. Compare the living death described by Walt Whitman as he looked with compassion at the body of a poor woman whose giddy, frivolous life was over, knowing that physical death was only the end of a dying she had been doing for years, he said:

Dead house of love—house of madness and sin, crumpled, crush'd,
House of life, erewhile talking and laughing—but ah, poor house,
   dead even then,
Months, years, an echoing garnish'd house—but dead, dead, dead! [9]

How much better to go to the great death of self-surrender and trust so that when the great physical death occurs, there will still be great life. I have known several who lived such great lives. At the time of their deaths the words of Roselle Montgomery on the death of an aged friend were entirely appropriate:

You are not dead—Life has but set you free!
· · · · · · · · · · · ·
For us who knew you, dread [of age] is past!
You took life, tiptoe, to the very last;
  It never lost for you its lovely look;
  You kept your interest in its thrilling book;
To you Death came no conqueror; in the end—
You merely smiled to greet another friend! [10]

This is *great* life meeting *great* death, and we believe it leads us to *greater* life. Such faith enables us to say with Alexis Baron von Ronne, the fine German Christian, who just before being hanged by the Nazis wrote to his wife, "In a moment I shall be going home to our Lord in complete calm and in the certainty of salvation . . . If you only knew with what inconceivable loyalty He is standing by my side at this moment, you would be armored and calm for all your difficult life. He will give you strength for anything." [11]

Here is, indeed, great life in death! The power to love others, even to the last, in calm victory. Call this illusion or wishful thinking, if you will—I call it deepest reality!

THE POWER OF GREAT FAITH

How does the acceptance by faith of the resurrection of Christ conquer the little deaths with their disease and decay, as well as the great death at the conclusion of our physical life?

Not by giving us "a chart, a map correct of heaven," of whatever is in store for us after death. We have no picture of the future life, nor any kind of description that is authentic, since no one has been there to return. As Jesus said in the parable of Dives and Lazarus, when Dives, the rich man in hell, asked Abraham to let him return to warn his brothers: "If they do not hear Moses and the prophets, neither will they be convinced if someone should rise from the dead" (Luke 16:31).

The pictures of heaven in Revelation are purely symbolic— the "golden streets" and "harps" were scarcely intended to be accepted literally!

No, our faith in Christ does not give us proof, so that we

149

know what is beyond death. If we "knew" there would be no need of faith—and everybody, out of expediency, would seek to be a disciple. There would be no real goodness. We would be a world of fawning robots, not of believing children.

> We have but faith: we cannot know,
> For knowledge is of things we see;
> And yet we trust it comes from thee,
> A beam in darkness: let it grow.[12]

It is faith-knowledge, as Paul describes it, that Christ gives us: "For I am convinced that neither death nor life . . . nor anything else in all creation, will be able to separate us from the love of God in Christ Jesus our Lord" (Rom. 8:35).

The little deaths-in-life and death itself are conquered by Christ, who in his resurrection gives us an assurance of the Love of God for us—a love that is wise and strong enough to include judgment on the evil, but wide and merciful enough to bring also a salvation, a healing of our estrangement, a hope for our present and future.

The only real basis for hope in life and death is the loving concern of God for us! As D. T. Niles, the Indian Christian, put it so beautifully: "Across the face of life is written the signature of death. But it is a signature that has been crossed out. And on the cross we see another signature, God's signature of love." [13]

There are at least four ways in which both kinds of death are challenged by the love of God as seen in the Resurrection of Christ:

First, *the love of God is more than a match for our human self-centeredness with its grief and despair.* How many times

I have witnessed this fact in the way Christians meet their
grief over the loss of dear ones! When I was in Bolivia in 1955,
I was a guest in the home of the Rev. and Mrs. Murray Dickson in Cochabamba. A fearless leader of Methodist Christians
in Bolivia, Murray Dickson's life even then was tremendous in
its influence. About nine years later I received word that he
was killed riding in a jeep on a narrow mountain road in central
Bolivia. His wife, Nova, returned to the United States with
her three children. I wrote her my sympathy, and received
word of her triumphant faith. She was going to school again
to prepare herself to go back and take up Murray's work. The
next Christmas I received this Christmas card from her from
Bolivia: "Murray lives today in the Universal Mission of the
World Church. He has always believed in the communion of
its members, and he has been right. We thank you for being
a part of this great fellowship with us and in this time of his
new appointment I know we will continue with him in his
work." What a victory over self-centeredness her faith brought.

Second, *God's love calls us to live again in the sharing of
his works of love—and thereby defeats our discouragement
and frustration.* Murray Dickson's "new appointment" was
greater than the old.

Among the many personal witnesses of this truth I have
known, perhaps one of the most inspiring is that of Charles
and Geneva Mooney and their victory of faith and love after
the loss of their brilliant and gifted son, John. At the time of
his tragic death in an automobile accident, John was a high-
ranking senior at Ohio Wesleyan University and a leader in
our student fellowship as well as in his fraternity and other
school organizations. A closely knit family, they were cast

down into the depths of grief; but out of it came stronger character and a remarkable love that enable them to spend many hours every week as counselors of a youth group.

They died with John but are living again in the sharing of the works of love with Christ in a ministry to a hundred young people who think of them as a second "Mom" and "Dad"!

"Therefore, my beloved brethren, be steadfast, immovable, always abounding in the work of the Lord, knowing that in the Lord your labor is not in vain" (I Cor. 15:58).

Third, *in the love of God as seen in the Risen Christ we know we may share "the communion of the saints" that takes the sting out of parting with dear ones.* The "saints" are "God's men and women"—ordinary men and women such as you and I, who having learned how to live, share now a greater life than we can imagine.

Mary Lecomte du Nuöy, in *Road to Human Destiny*, tells of her last hours with her distinguished husband, scientist, biologist, and Christian, who had done so much to show that science and the Christian faith are not contradictory. They had planned many things together. But now seriously ill, Pierre asked her to continue their work. She answered that she could do nothing without him, and he said, "Oh, yes, you can, I will help you. I promise I will help you. . . . Nothing can ever separate us, do you hear me? *Nothing!*" [14]

He could say this because through much doubt and struggle he had come to believe that nothing could separate him or her from the love of Christ. Therefore, nothing could separate them from each other. In what way I do not know, but the communion of the saints is real. Therefore the sting is removed from parting. We cannot see them, yet we know their influence is with us and their lives are with God. With him we leave them and in him we trust.

Fourth, *our love for God through Christ enables us to accept ourselves as loved by God, to accept ourselves and to love others in God's love for us that makes life eternal.* "This is life eternal to know Him." Mary in the garden that morning knew him when he called her name. His love made God's love real.

Two old fears were dispelled on that first
    Easter morning:
That dark death marked defeat and the end of
    human striving;
That great God held himself far aloof from our
    mourning.
Are there tears of concern in the heart of
    the Eternal?
Is there hope that man's life is not vainly
    forgotten?
Does God care, does he know when our hearts are
    all broken?
Yes, "God raised him to life, set him free from
    death's destruction!"
God said, "Mary!" She said, "Master!" In that
    Divine Encounter
All may know that the heart of the Eternal
    has a kindness
No man's thoughts can measure! God is suff'ring through
    our agony!
So God raises us to life e'en in death with
    its destruction!
God does care! Knowing this, what can threaten
    or defeat us?

Knowing this, through a commitment of living faith in Christ our Lord, let us begin in this moment a great life that conquers even the little deaths as well as the big death. Let us in this moment begin that life which will continue and grow greater until "morning breaks and the shadows flee away."

NOTES

I. the LOSS of MY AUTHENTIC SELF

1. E. Sanford Martin, "My Name is Legion," *Masterpieces of Religious Verse*, ed. James Dalton Morrison (New York: Harper & Brothers, 1948), p. 274.
2. Robert Ruark, *Poor No More* (New York: Henry Holt and Company, 1959).
3. William Saroyan, *The Human Comedy* (New York: Harcourt, Brace and Company, 1943), pp. 71-72.

II. DOING what COMES NATURALLY

1. Mark Twain, "The Damned Human Race," in *Letters from the Earth* (New York: Harper & Row, 1962).
2. George Bernard Shaw, *Sixteen Self Sketches* (New York: Dodd, Mead & Co., 1949).
3. David Head, *He Sent Leanness* (New York: The Macmillan Company, 1959), p. 50.
4. Pierre Teilhard de Chardin, *The Phenomenon of Man* (New York: Harper Torchbooks, 1961), p. 191.
5. Pierre Lecomte du Nuöy, *Human Destiny* (New York: Longmans, Green, 1947), p. 195.
6. Oscar Wilde, *A Woman of No Importance*, Act III.
7. From *Modern Humor for Effective Speaking* by Edward Frank Allen. Copyright 1945 by Edward Frank Allen. Published by Dover Publications, Inc., New York 14, N.Y. and reprinted through permission of the publisher.
8. T. S. Eliot, "The Hollow Men," from *Collected Poems 1909-1962*. Used by permission of Harcourt, Brace & World, Inc. and Faber and Faber Ltd.
9. John Gillespie Magee, Jr., "High Flight," from *Masterpieces of Religious Verse*, p. 73. Reprinted by permission of Harper & Row, Publishers.

155

10. Archibald MacLeish, *J.B.* (Boston: Houghton Mifflin, 1958), p. 17.
11. Emil Brunner, *Christian Doctrine of Creation and Redemption* (Philadelphia: Westminster Press, 1952), pp. 338-39.
12. Vance Packard, *The Waste Makers* (New York: David McKay Company, 1960), pp. 53-77.

III. SET FREE to CARE

1. A more complete treatment of the difference between possessing and giving love and its results and the meaning of love as made possible by an acceptance of ourselves as loved by God is to be found in Lance Webb, *Discovering Love* (Nashville: Abingdon Press, 1959).
2. MacLeish, *J.B.*, p. 11.
3. Albert Camus, *The Rebel* (New York: Vintage Books, 1957), p. 58.
4. *Ibid.*, p. 248.
5. *Ibid.*, pp. 304-5.
6. Aldous Huxley, *Tomorrow and Tomorrow and Tomorrow* (New York: Harper & Row, 1956).
7. Emil Ludwig, *Napoleon* (New York: Boni & Liveright, 1926), p. 598.
8. James Moffatt, *Love in the New Testament* (New York: Richard R. Smith, Inc., 1930), p. 44.
9. C. S. Lewis, *The Four Loves* (New York: Harcourt, Brace and World, 1960), p. 163.
10. Ernest Gordon, *Through the Valley of the Kwai* (New York: Harper & Row, 1962), p. 75.
11. *Ibid.*, pp. 163-64.
12. Kathryn Hulme, *The Nun's Story* (Boston: Little, Brown & Co., 1956), p. 240.
13. George Matheson, "O Love That Wilt Not Let Me Go."
14. Isaac Watts, "When I Survey the Wondrous Cross."

IV. the ABSURDITY of UNBELIEF

1. John Baillie, *Our Knowledge of God* (New York: Charles Scribner's Sons, 1959), pp. 42-53.
2. Fanny Heaslip Lea, "The Dead Faith," used by permission of Harold Ober Associates, Incorporated.
3. W. Somerset Maugham, *Of Human Bondage* (Garden City, N.Y.: Doubleday & Co., 1942), p. 401.
4. *Ibid.*, p. 655.
5. Camus, *The Rebel*, p. 57.
6. William Adams Brown, "Ways of Reaching Certainty," *The Fellowship of the Saints*, ed. Thomas S. Kepler (Nashville: Abingdon Press 1958), p. 641.

7. *Ibid.*
8. Camus, *The Rebel*, pp. 25, 58, 60-61, 71, 76, 78.
9. The author is indebted to Karl Heim in *Christian Faith and Natural Science* (Gloucester, Mass.: Peter Smith, Publisher, 1961), for use of the terms "extreme relativism" and "positivism" in this connection.
10. From "Dance" by James Stephens. Reprinted with the permission of The Macmillan Company from *Collected Poems* by James Stephens, copyright 1912 by The Macmillan Company. Renewed 1944 by James Stephens.
11. Emil Brunner, *God and Man*, trans. David Cairns (London: Student Christian Movement Press, 1936), p. 155.

V. FINDING the GOALPOSTS

1. "Morals: The Second Sexual Revolution," *Time* (January 24, 1964), pp. 54-55.
2. Sherwood Eddy, *I Have Seen God Do It* (New York: Harper & Brothers, 1940), p. 57.
3. MacLeish, *J.B.*, p. 108.
4. Viktor Frankl, *Man's Search for Meaning* (New York: Washington Square Press, 1963), p. 183.
5. Charles Darwin, *Origin of Species* (Philadelphia: University of Pennsylvania Press, 1958), p. 421.
6. Quoted in J. Wallace Hamilton, "Slipping Feet," *The Pulpit* (November 11, 1951), p. 8.
7. Hugh Hefner, "The Playboy Philosophy," from editorials appearing in the 1963-64 issues of *Playboy*.
8. Edward Fitzgerald (trans.), "The Rubaiyat of Omar Khayyam."
9. John Donne, *Devotions*, XVII.
10. Paul Tournier, *Guilt and Grace* (New York: Harper & Row, 1962), p. 78.
11. James Russell Lowell, "Once to Every Man and Nation."
12. Paul Tillich, *Morality and Beyond* (New York: Harper & Row, 1963), p. 42.

VI. HOPE and the COURAGE to LIVE

1. Charles Pierre Péguy, *God Speaks*, trans. Julian Green (New York: Pantheon Books, Inc., 1945).
2. William Ernest Henley, "Invictus."
3. Henry Sloane Coffin, *Communion Through Preaching* (New York: Charles Scribner's Sons, 1952), p. 47.
4. Cyril Richardson (ed.), *Early Christian Fathers* "The Library of Christian Classics" (Philadelphia: Westminster Press, 1953), I, 213.
5. William Shakespeare, *Hamlet*, Act III, Sc. I.

6. William Shakespeare, *King Lear*, Act II, Sc. IV.
7. Elizabeth Barrett Browning, "A Vision of Poets."
8. Antoine de Saint-Exupery, *Night Flight*, trans. Stuart Gilbert (New York: The Century Co., 1932).
9. Nobel Prize Acceptance Speech.
10. William Wordsworth, "Valedictory Sonnet to the River Duddon."

VII. LIFE in DEATH

1. Markus Barth and Verne H. Fletcher, *Acquittal by Resurrection* (New York: Holt, Rinehart & Winston, 1964), pp. 25-26.
2. *Ibid.*, p. 13.
3. Quoted by Arthur S. Link, *Woodrow Wilson: The New Freedom* (Princeton, N.J.: Princeton University Press, 1956), pp. 64-65.
4. Leo Tolstoy, *Confession*, trans. Aylmer Maude (New York: Oxford University Press).
5. Ruark, *Poor No More*, p. 611.
6. Nicholas Berdyaev, *Destiny of Man* (New York: Harper & Row, 1960), p. 320.
7. From "A Metropolis" by Don Marquis, copyright 1915 by Sun Printing & Publishing Assn. From the book *Poems and Portraits* by Don Marquis. Reprinted by permission of Doubleday & Company, Inc.
8. G. Elsie Harrison, *Son to Susanna* (Nashville: Cokesbury Press, 1938), p. 207.
9. Walt Whitman, "The City Dead-House."
10. Roselle Mercier Montgomery, "On the Death of an Aged Friend," from *Masterpieces of Religious Verse*, p. 586. Reprinted by permission of Harper & Row, Publishers.
11. Helmut Gollwitzer and others, *Dying We Live*, trans. Reinhard C. Kuhn (New York: Pantheon Books, 1956), p. 284.
12. Alfred Lord Tennyson, "In Memoriam."
13. D. T. Niles, *Preaching the Gospel of the Resurrection* (Philadelphia: Westminster Press, 1954), p. 74.
14. Mary Lecomte du Nuöy, *Road to Human Destiny*, p. 298.